Kitchen Stories Cookbook
Comfort Cookin'
Made Fascinating and Easy

**Linda Altoonian
and
Lael Morgan**

Epicenter Press
Kenmore, Washington

Epicenter Press
6524 NE 181st Street #2
Kenmore, WA 98028
www.epicenterpress.com

Epicenter Press is a regional house publishing nonfiction books about the arts, history, environment, and diverse cultures and lifestyles of Alaska and the Pacific Northwest.

Copyright © 2015 Linda Altoonian and Lael Morgan

All rights reserved. No part of this publication may be reproduced, stored in a retrieval system, or transmitted in any form or by any means, electronic, mechanical, photocopying, recording, or otherwise, without prior written permission of the publisher. Permission is given for brief excerpts to be published with book reviews in newspapers, magazines, newsletters, catalogs, and online publications.

Trademarks are used in text of this book for informational purposes only, and no affiliation with or endorsement by the trademark owners is claimed or suggested.

Cover and chapter openings photos and design by Lauren Taylor and Linda Altoonian.

Website Design by Madeleine Dao of Arlington, Texas.
www.kitchenstoriescookbook.blogspot.com

Softcover ISBN: 978-1-935347-44-6
Hardcover ISBN: 978-1-935347-71-2
Library of Congress Control Number 201560540
10 9 8 7 6 5 4 3 2 1

Printed in Canada

TABLE OF CONTENTS

Foreword v

Introduction: Comfort Cookin' vii

Appetizers 1

Bread and Rolls 21

Salads 37

    Salad Dressings 52

Soups, Stews, and Chowders 59

Entrées 75

    Gravy, Sauces, and Toppings 121

Vegetables and Side Dishes 131

Desserts 159

    Dessert Sauces 189

    Frostings and Icings 194

Drinks 201

Acknowledgments 209

Appendix: Foodie Autobiographies 211

Recipe Index 223

Contact Information 227

FOREWORD

Not until my physician diagnosed me as diabetic did I develop a genuine interest in food. Please understand, I've always loved to eat, but in that BD (before diabetes) part of my life, I ate promiscuously. Pie, candy, turnovers, cinnamon rolls, fast food, you name it: if it looked or smelled good, I pounced on it. Then, with remarkable suddenness, I had to terminate my pernicious affair with sugar. Perforce, I became more discriminating in my food choices. It was then, that my wife Deborah and I discovered historic dining.

On a trip to Philadelphia, Deb visited City Tavern and discovered the joys of eighteenth-century cooking. So impressed was she, that she purchased Chef Walter Staib's City Tavern Cookbook: *200 Years of Classic Recipes from America's First Gourmet Restaurant*. What a revelation. History had always fascinated me, but Chef Staib taught me that what our ancestors ate—and how they prepared it—defined them as much as (probably more than) how they voted, how they fought, and how they dressed. Consider how much of what people eat, where they eat, and how they eat characterizes their "lifestyle"—however one chooses to define that reprehensible expression.

I began incorporating preparation of historic recipes into the curriculum. I required that my students prepare a selection from Chef Staib's cookbook and then participate in colonial dinners that Deb and I hosted. The assignment spawned much hand wringing and teeth gnashing; students carp when their professors hurl them out of their comfort zones. Do it anyway. Before sitting down to dine, students explained what they had experienced during the preparation of each dish. While not every venture was equally successful, each was, at least, eatable. The most common comment was, "I've never tasted anything like this—but I like it." Students began to grasp that their ancestors were different from them. If we who occupy the present are to understand the past, we must come to terms with those variations. When my students duplicated historic recipes, they learned how different their forebears were. They also discovered that their food choices were just as valid as theirs, and just as good. In addition, to the food, Deb and I attempted to create an eighteenth-century setting. It was the first time many of these young people had ever dined by candlelight. Notwithstanding all the bellyaching beforehand, almost all of them confessed that the colonial dinner had been the most memorable, and edifying, portion of the class.

This book excites me. Linda and Lael have provided a wonderful resource for period cooks. The recipes are simplicity itself (and blessedly many of them are sugar free), but I confess the stories that accompany them are more to my interest. Socrates observed, "The unexamined life is not worth living." I would further allow that unexamined food is not worth eating. Anyone can jot down recipes, but, by providing the anecdotes behind the food, the authors add to our understanding—and enjoyment—of it. At its core, history is simply the long chronicle of our humanity. And what could be a more human experience than a meal prepared by loving hands, shared with friends and family. That is why such moments linger so long in our memories. Linda and Lael have detailed their family recipes, but more important they have shared their stories, their memories, and their humanity.

Stephen L. Hardin, Ph.D.
History Professor, McMurry University

INTRODUCTION

Comfort Cookin': Why Comfort Food Is a Joy

Exploring and honoring our heritage through a favorite recipe (comfort foods or soul foods) can be a delicious experience. Dishes like New England baked beans, Grandma's macaroni and cheese, and chicken soup like Mother used to make can often brighten a bad day, soothe a singed soul, and even cure some physical ills. Valuing our past also provides us with a sense of security and continuity in an era of turbulence and rapid change, and favorite ethnic dishes remind us of our roots and traditions.

Lifestyle changes—just growing up or being away from home for the first or last time, the loss of a partner, divorce, recovery from a serious disease, and the empty-nest syndrome—are always challenging. So is constantly being on the run, perhaps as a soccer mom, for business trips or retirement travel.

Challenges of various kinds and hectic schedules can make fixing food the last thing we want to do when we get home. What once was a pleasurable activity that enabled us to be creative and allowed us to demonstrate our love to others often evolves into yet another unsavory chore.

That is why we created this delightful collection of favorite Comfort Food recipes that need *only* six ingredients (or fewer)! Each recipe serves four diners and requires only the most basic utensils. Some recipes are updated with a modern twist or intriguing variation but are still easy to make, even for those who have never cooked before. Yet sophisticated cooks will appreciate this historical collection, too, because of the speed and ease with which these dishes can be prepared without the sacrifice of fine, full flavor that made them a treasured recipe in the first place.

Your Authors' Stories are Unique

Before you read further, it might help if we explain that we are two professional writers who, between us, have explored most of the world, eaten in most of the best restaurants, and learned some great techniques from some of the best chefs. We both worked many years as journalists. We both teach. We both love to entertain, experiment in the kitchen, and will eat and cook just about anything. And we are most protective of the traditional recipes on which we were raised.

We are also different in ways that make our collaboration unique. To highlight our varied experiences, we have introduced each recipe with a story. Some are poignant; some are funny, and some give fascinating historical information about the dish. We hope our "Kitchen Stories" will entertain, inform and even remind you of some of your own sweet, funny or even crazy stories about cooking in the kitchen with the people you love.

Note: In the name of complete disclosure—you'll find "foodie" autobiographies by each of us in the Appendix of this cookbook.

APPETIZERS

"Flavorful, festive, and fun, the appetizer is often the most tantalizing part of any food event. Whether crunchy, creamy, or stick-to-the-roof-of-your-mouth chewy, the appetizer is a little bite of heaven—especially when the recipe is simple.

"If you get bored with regular meals, consider dining just on hors d'oeuvres. You might feel slightly wicked, but you will also create a party atmosphere that can prove fun." Linda

Artichoke Dip

"Corn chips or Harvest 5 Grain Crackers are perfect dippers for this hot treat." Linda

Ingredients

2, 14 oz. cans of artichoke hearts, drained and chopped
4 oz. grated Parmesan cheese
1 cup mayonnaise
¼ tsp. garlic salt
¼ tsp. Worcestershire Sauce
¼ tsp. hot sauce (optional)

Directions

1. Preheat oven to 350°. **2.** Combine ingredients as listed, stirring well after adding each ingredient. **3.** Spoon into lightly greased, 1 qt. casserole. **4.** Bake for 20 minutes.

Bruschetta Cheddar

"There is nothing more delicious than a bite of something that is crisp and gooey. This is Italy's answer." Linda

Ingredients

24 slices French bread (¾ inch thick)
2 medium tomatoes, seeded and chopped
⅔ cup shredded cheddar cheese
⅓ cup mayonnaise
¼ cup grated Parmesan cheese
½ teaspoon dried basil

Additions: ½ tsp. oregano, ½ tsp. black pepper

Directions

1. Place bread slices on ungreased baking sheets. Bake at 350° for 5 minutes on each side or until toasted. **2.** Combine the remaining ingredients. Spread over toasted bread. Bake 8–10 minutes longer or until bubbly. Serve warm.

Cheese Ball

"The author of Great Balls of Cheese, *Michelle Buffardi, says that according to legend, the first cheese ball was created in 1801 by farmer Elisha Brown, Jr. and presented to President Thomas Jefferson at the White House. It was called "mammoth cheese" because it weighed 1,235 pounds. Though Lael and I also consider the cheese ball an excellent hostess gift and a delicious hors d'oeuvre, we recommend a far smaller size rolled in nuts and served with crackers, celery sticks, and a serving knife."* Linda

Ingredients
8 oz. bleu cheese
8 oz. cream cheese
½ cup butter
1 T. chives
6 oz. chopped black olives
6 oz. chopped pecans
   or walnuts

Directions
1. Allow cheeses and butter to soften. **2.** Mix all ingredients except nuts and form into a ball. **3.** Roll the formed ball in the nuts.

Easy Cheese

"Want to tantalize your guests with both sweet and spicy? Try this scrumptious appetizer." Linda

Ingredients
12 ounce log of goat cheese
2 T. mixed herbs of choice
   (dill, basil, oregano)
1 T. cashews, chopped
1 T. cranberries, chopped
1 T. mixed peppercorns
Toasted baguette slices or
   salted crackers

Directions
1. Cut goat cheese crosswise into 3 mini logs. **2.** Roll 1 piece in mixed, chopped herbs, another in the cracked, mixed peppercorns, and the last in finely chopped, dried cranberries and cashews. **3.** Serve with toasted baguette slices or salted crackers.

Chicken Wings Buffalo

"The city of Buffalo officially decreed July 29, 1977, to be Chicken Wing Day. Word of this upper state New York recipe has since spread to a point that there are shops that specialize in spicy wings all over our nation. This is a simple recipe and its success is partly in the sauce in which you dip this appetizer. Bleu cheese dressing is a classic, but there are many other choices." Lael

Ingredients
2 lbs. chicken wings
3 cups cooking oil
1 T. hot pepper sauce
¼ cup melted butter
¼ cup bleu cheese
½ cup sour cream

Additions: 1 clove garlic, minced, 1 tsp. Worcestershire Sauce, and mayonnaise to taste.

Directions
1. Cut off wing tips and split each into two pieces at the joint.
2. Put 2" of oil in a heavy 4-quart saucepan and heat to 375° (just short of smoking hot). Lower the wings into oil and fry for 15 minutes or until tender. Drain on paper towel. **3.** Blend pepper sauce and butter together in a large bowl. Toss in chicken wings and coat them with the mixture. **4.** Serve with dip made with bleu cheese mixed with sour cream, garlic, Worcestershire Sauce, and mayonnaise.

Variation
After cooking wings, roll them in Parmesan cheese and serve.

Chicken Wings Far East

"This recipe was given to me by a friend who grew up in Kauai, Hawaii, where there is a large influx of Japanese tourists. From them, Carla learned to make white rice a tempting dish to eat and these succulent chicken wings. The very first time she served this appetizer, I was hooked." Linda

Ingredients
12 chicken wings
½ cup soy sauce
1 cup scallions, chopped
1 tsp. sugar
1 tsp. powdered ginger

Directions
1. Cut off wing tips and split each into two pieces at the joint. **2.** Mix remaining ingredients and pour over wings. **3.** Cover and refrigerate overnight. Add more soy sauce if necessary. **4.** Bake for 15 minutes in 350° oven.

Dill Dip

"Dill weed is one of my favorite herbs. It is aromatic and delicious in and on all kinds of dishes, and it is extremely good for us. It contains chemical compounds that are anti-oxidant and disease preventing, and it can help in controlling blood cholesterol levels, so add it liberally, because it is also low in calories. This dip/sauce that I concocted is delicious with fresh vegetables, and with fish, especially salmon." Linda

Ingredients
1 cup sour cream
¼ cup mayonnaise (optional)
1 T. dried or fresh dill
1 T. onions, minced
1 tsp. Lawry's garlic salt
¼ tsp. pepper

Directions
1. Mix ingredients together and refrigerate.

Clam Dip

"*I was not a fan of anything raw, but my uncles just loved clams that way. Although intrigued, I would always decline trying them because they looked too much like raw eggs. Though I still don't like clams raw, I do love clams that swim in the cream of a great chowder, in garlic butter over pasta, and in the broth of a great gumbo.*

"*My dad's brothers, uncles Dick and Deran, were the first to introduce me to a number of exotic sea dwellers. Because our home on that side of the family was in Providence, Rhode Island, we spent a lot of time at the sea shore when we visited them.*

"*These uncles were also the ones who taught me gin rummy and gave me one of the most beautiful side tables I own. I'm sure it dates back to the days of Paul Revere, but I don't want to know for sure because I wouldn't give it up for all the money in the world. Looking at it reminds me of how important the two of those uncles were to me.*

"*Their recipe below for this delicious clam dip can be served with chips, crackers, and/or fresh vegetables.*" Linda

Ingredients

6.5 oz. can clams, minced (reserve the juice)
3 oz. pkg. cream cheese, softened
1 T. scallions or onions, diced
½ tsp. Worcestershire Sauce

Directions

1. Drain clams except 1 T. of juice. **2.** Soften the cream cheese and mix in the juice. **3.** Beat onions and sauce into cream cheese. **4.** Mix in clams and refrigerate for several hours. **5.** Serve with chips, crackers and vegetables.

Variation

Replace cream cheese with 1 cup sour cream and add ½ tsp. salt, ¼ tsp. pepper, and ½ tsp. garlic powder.

Crab Dip

"You would think that after packing crab for two seasons, I wouldn't like it anymore, but, in truth, I am addicted. The Seldovia, Alaska, cannery where I worked only partially cooked the meat before it was put in the cans. The crab-loaded conveyer belt stopped under the cooker and heated that straight-from-the-sea king crab so it was just perfect to nibble on during our coffee breaks. We considered striking for butter to go with it, but thought better of that idea. Crab is, however, delicious with melted butter or in a good dip. You can also add cooked crab to our Feta Spread recipe." Lael

Ingredients

4¼ oz. can crabmeat or 1 pkg. frozen crab meat
8 oz. pkg. cream cheese, softened
1 T. garlic salt
½ T. Worcestershire Sauce
¼ tsp. white pepper
crackers (Triscuits are great with this)

Directions

1. Mix cream cheese with crabmeat. **2.** Add garlic salt and Worcestershire Sauce. **3.** Add pepper. **4.** Microwave until hot. Mix again before serving with crackers.

Deviled Eggs

"The word 'deviled,' used as a cooking term in the 18th Century, usually referred to a dish that was spicy. If a family preferred not to make reference to the devil, they would call this still-popular appetizer "Angel Eggs." Those who grew up in the south may have heard them called "stuffed" or "salad" eggs." Lael

Ingredients

6 eggs
¼ cup mayonnaise
1 tsp. prepared mustard (optional)
½ tsp. salt (for water in which to boil eggs)
½ tsp. garlic salt
Paprika

Additions: 1 stalk celery, chopped fine, 1 small onion, minced, and/or a small dill pickle slice, chopped fine.

Directions

1. Place eggs in saucepan with enough cold water to cover. Bring to a boil over high heat. Then reduce heat so water is just below simmering and cook for 15 minutes. Drain and cover with cold water for two minutes. Crack each eggshell on countertop. Roll egg between palms of hands and peel off shell, starting at the large end. Cut each egg in half, lengthwise, and scoop yolk into a mixing bowl. **2.** Mash yolks with a fork. Stir in mayonnaise. Add mustard, celery, onion and pickle if desired. **3.** Pile yolk mixture into egg white centers. Refrigerate until serving time. Then sprinkle with paprika.

Feta Spread

"Feta cheese, made from sheep or goat's milk, is a staple in Mediterranean diets. It was always part of the "Mezze" served before our holiday dinners. Mezze is a spread of small appetizers that also features big Greek olives, hummus, pickled vegetables, and a couple of shots of strong drink (whiskey or brandy, drunk mostly by the men).

"Delicious on crackers, in sandwiches, and crumbled in salads, feta cheese is also high in saturated fat and sodium. Because it has such a bold and tangy flavor, using a little goes a long way." *Linda*

"My life became richer when I discovered feta cheese, which I use mostly for Greek Salad that I sometimes eat four times a week. Initially, I ignored this spread recipe that I found on a cheese container. Today, it is my most requested recipe, not only good for hors d'oeuvres, but also for topping baked potatoes and other vegetables." *Lael*

Ingredients

8 oz. crumbled feta cheese
8 oz. pkg. cream cheese, softened
2-4 T. olive oil
3 or more cloves of garlic, minced
¼ tsp. black pepper
Crackers or pita bread cut in pie-shaped pieces

Additions: ⅓ cup chopped black olives, 2 T. chopped green onions, and ⅓ cup cooked crabmeat and/or chopped parsley.

Directions

1. Remove cheeses from refrigerator and let stand until room temperature. **2.** Combine cheeses, olive oil, and garlic in a bowl, and mix together. If mixture is too stiff, add a bit more olive oil. **3.** Add black olives and/or crab, if desired, and mix. **4.** Top with parsley. **5.** Spread on pita bread slices or simply put out bread, crackers, and the feta spread, and let your guests do the work.

Phyllo Cheese

"Phyllo dough is a staple in Mediterranean and Middle Eastern cooking. Armenians (my nationality) and Greeks stuff it, layer it, and use it in both sweet and savory dishes, and, believe it or not, my grandmother used to make those paper thin sheets of dough from scratch! I can't begin to imagine the time and work that took. Today, lots of folks use that dough in all kinds of great hors d'oeuvres and desserts, and you can find it easily in the dessert freezer section of your grocery store." Linda

Ingredients

1 pkg. of Phyllo dough, defrosted in refrigerator overnight.
2 sticks of butter, melted

1 large container of large curd cottage cheese
1 pkg. cream cheese, softened
2 eggs, mixed
½ tsp. salt

Directions

1. In a bowl, mix softened cream cheese with cottage cheese. **2.** Add mixed eggs and salt and stir thoroughly to create the stuffing mix. **3.** Use a brush to butter bottom and sides of a 9 x 12" pan. **4.** Roll out Phyllo dough and add four sheets to pan. Brush the top sheet with butter. **5.** Repeat three more times and then add the filling and spread evenly over dough. **6.** Cover filling with four sheets of dough and butter top. Repeat until all dough is gone. **7.** Brush top layer with butter. **8. Critical:** Cut into pieces before baking. Use a sharp knife and cut lengthwise down the center, then each half in half. Turn pan and cut lengths into halves and quarters. **9.** Pour remaining butter over cuts. **10.** Bake in a 350° oven for about 20 minutes or until golden brown on top.

Guacamole

"My children tell me that my guacamole has spoiled them to other offerings, including at Mexican restaurants. Obviously, mine has no preservatives and is served right away, but the trick is to pulverize the onion so its juice is extracted into the bowl before adding the avocado. Then mash the two together with the garlic salt before adding the tomato. I do not add much of other flavors that can overpower the avocado. This recipe is not only delicious for dipping with Tortilla chips and Fritos, but it also makes a good topping for sandwiches, salads and other Mexican dishes." Linda

Ingredients

1 fully ripened avocado, halved, pitted, and peeled
1 chopped plum tomato
1 T. onion, minced
½ tsp. garlic salt
½ tsp. lemon juice (optional)
1 tsp. jalapeno pepper, chopped (optional)

Possible toppings: sour cream, cheddar cheese, green onions, garlic salt, pepper

Directions

1. Mash onion to extract juice and soften onion. **2.** Then mash avocado into the onion until slightly chunky. **3.** Add garlic salt. **4.** Stir in tomatoes with their juice. **5.** Add lemon juice (optional). **6.** Mix in jalapeno pepper. Serve immediately or, if is to be stored for some time in the refrigerator, put the avocado pit into the mixture and add a light coating of mayonnaise to keep the guacamole from turning brown.

Hummus Dip

"Chick peas, also known as garbanzo beans, are rich in zinc, folate, and protein, and are low in fat. Grown in the Mediterranean, western Asia, and the Indian subcontinent, chickpeas can be cooked in stews or eaten cold in salads, ground into a flour, fermented to make an alcoholic drink similar to sake, stirred into a batter and baked, cooked and ground into a paste called hummus, or roasted, spiced, and eaten as a snack. Hummus is a power food that should be served with pita chips or fresh pita bread cut into triangles." *Linda*

"Linda makes it sound as if chickpeas are good for you which, for some of us, takes away all the joy. However, friends and I have yet to recover when, during her recent trip to visit me in Alaska, she casually mixed up a batch of this stuff, and we were hooked. Don't let the simplicity of this recipe fool you. It's wonderful!" *Lael*

Ingredients

- 16 oz. can chickpeas, drained and rinsed
- 1/4 cup onion, any color including green, diced
- 1/4 cup olive oil
- 1 tsp. lemon juice (more if you'd like it tangier)
- 1 tsp. garlic salt
- 1 tsp. pepper

Directions

1. Put all ingredients into a blender or processor and blend until smooth. **2.** Pour into shaped bowl or platter. **3.** Drizzle some olive oil on top. **4.** Sprinkle with paprika and garnish with fresh parsley. **5.** Serve with pita chips or fresh pita bread cut into triangles.

Variations

1. 3 T. sesame paste, also called tahini, with fresh parsley as a garnish. **2.** Use black beans instead of chickpeas.

Mexican Layered Dip

"Serve with tortilla, corn, or pita chips." Linda
"And just pile the leftovers on a baked potato." Lael

Ingredients

Guacamole dip (already featured)
1 can refried bean dip
1 cup sour cream
½ cup mayonnaise
1.25 oz. pkg. taco seasoning mix
3 medium tomatoes, chopped

Additions: green onions, pitted black olives, sharp cheddar cheese

Directions

1. Spread bean dip on large, shallow serving platter. **2.** Spread guacamole on top of bean dip but allow the bean dip to show around the edges. **3.** Combine sour cream, mayonnaise, and taco mix and spread onto guacamole but allow green of guacamole to show. **4.** Chop up tomatoes and cover sour cream mixture. **5.** Sprinkle with green onions, black olives, and cheese.

Mini Lasagna

"I adore traditional lasagna but when life gets busy, I can't always muster the get-up-and-go to manufacture it. This mini-substitute doesn't take much time or money, and it can be a meal in itself as well as an exciting appetizer." Lael

Ingredients

1 pkg. of wonton wrappers (usually in major supermarkets)
1 jar marinara sauce
1 carton ricotta cheese
Pesto (recipe in Index)
Cooking spray

Directions

1. Heat oven to 375° with rack in middle position. **2.** Coat 12 muffin cups evenly with cooking spray. **3.** Line each cup with a wonton wrapper (corners will stick out). **4.** Fill with 1 T. marinara sauce, 1 tsp. ricotta, and ¼ tsp. pesto. **5.** Repeat a second layer if your wonton wrappers are big enough. **6.** Lightly coat edges of wonton wrappers with cooking spray. **7.** Bake until edges are golden brown and filling is heated through (about 10 minutes). **8.** Let stand in muffin pan 1 to 2 minutes before removing with spoon (or fingers) and transferring to plates.

Note: Standard sizes of each ingredient will produce two batches of this nifty cocktail food.

Nachos

"I knew nothing about Mexican food when I moved to California in 1969. Soon I became a fan of Taco Bell with its outdoor fire ring in Laguna Beach. 'It can't get much better than this,' I decided, so I was stunned when co-workers introduced me to El Adobe in San Juan Capistrano, where President Richard Nixon also liked to dine. "*It was here that I discovered truly delicious Mexican food, especially Nachos. The first batch I tried to make on my own caught fire and nearly burned out my kitchen. Even so, nachos remain not only a favorite appetizer but one of my favorite suppers."* Lael

"I spent one glorious summer, also in 1969, living in Los Angeles with my sister Diana. I worked for an insurance company with the best cafeteria in the world. The chefs were all Hispanic and cooked the most delicious Mexican food I had ever tasted. None of us ever left the building for lunch elsewhere because the food was just that good. When I returned home to Maryland, I searched for a comparable Mexican restaurant. Each attempt ended in disappointment and heartburn until George Bush became President of the United States. With his inauguration, finally came the opening of fabulous Tex-Mex restaurants in the Washington, D.C., area where I grew up." Linda

Ingredients

13 oz. pkg. of tortilla chips
1 ½ cup grated cheddar cheese and/or Monterey jack
2 green onions, chopped
Salsa (recipe page 17)
Sour cream

Additions: sliced jalapeños, chopped tomatoes, diced green pepper, and/or black olives cut in little rings.

Directions

1. Spread chips out on a greased cookie sheet and sprinkle with cheese. Bake in oven at 325° until cheese melts and begins to brown. (**Warning:** If you try broiling and place the chips too close to heating element, your nachos will catch fire.) **2.** Remove from oven and add toppings. Serve immediately.

Salmon Mousse

"By late August, most Alaskan refrigerators contain so many salmon you have to kick in their tails to close the door. As a newcomer to Alaska in 1959, I came in second at the National Pillsbury Bake-off competition with a salmon recipe I invented to diminish the glut. However, having eaten nothing but salmon for forty-seven days in a row while researching a book on Bristol Bay, where much of the world's supply is netted, I don't ever want to think about that fish again. Yes, I still like an occasional taste of it, but I left it to Linda to submit this elegant dip recipe." Lael

Ingredients

6 oz. can of salmon
8 oz. pkg. cream cheese, softened
½ tsp. lemon juice
1 tsp. onion flakes or fresh onion, diced
½ tsp. garlic salt
Ritz crackers

Directions

1. Mix ingredients together and shape into a log or pour into a fish mold. **2.** Refrigerate until firm. **3.** Serve with Ritz crackers.

Salsa

"My son, Derek, has become a great cook who serves up healthy fare that is creative, colorful, and delicious. He has been a salsa fan since he was two years old when, before we could stop him, he dipped a chip into the hottest sauce on the table and ate it. We screamed and so did he ... for more. He loved salsa then and loves it still in a variety of dishes he's created, including scrambled eggs with Parmesan cheese, now also my favorite way to eat them.

"This versatile sauce can totally replace ketchup (which avoids all that sugar) in most dishes. Add it to browned beef and vegetables, meatloaf, soups, and chili." Linda

Ingredients

16 oz. can Italian-style plum tomatoes or 3 large fresh tomatoes, peeled and seeded

4 oz. can mild or hot green chilies, drained

1 small onion, chopped

1 small clove garlic, chopped

3 T. fresh parsley leaves

Hot pepper sauce to taste

Additions: ¼ tsp. red pepper, seeded, and/or dash of ground coriander, one whole green onion, chopped, and/or ¼ cup cilantro, chopped.

Directions

1. Put tomatoes, chilies, onion, and garlic into food processor or blender. Whiz until coarsely chopped. Add parsley and coriander. Process just enough to mix. **2.** Add hot pepper sauce to taste. **3.** Can use immediately or refrigerate, covered, up to three days.

Shrimp Dip

"I was given this recipe by my best friend of forty-five years. Barb, who lives in Florida where I was born, and I love all things shrimp. Serve this delicious dip with vegetables or sweet crackers like Ritz." Linda

Ingredients
8 oz. pkg. cream cheese, softened
3 T. chili sauce
½ tsp. minced onion
⅓ cup mayonnaise
2 tsp. lemon juice (optional)
1 medium can of shrimp, fresh could also be used.

Directions
1. Combine all but shrimp and mix thoroughly. **2.** Add shrimp and refrigerate.

Tortilla Roll-ups

"These are made best with flour tortillas that are fresh and soft." Linda

Ingredients
8 oz. pkg. cream cheese, softened
¼ cup milk
3 tsp. garlic salt
1 green pepper, diced
1 red onion, diced
8 flour tortillas

Additions: ¼ cup chopped ham, ¼ cup diced pimento

Directions
1. Mix softened cream cheese with milk. **2.** Add garlic salt. **3.** Add vegetables and pimento. **4.** Spread a thin layer on a tortilla and roll up. **5.** Slice the roll into ¼" slices.

Texas Caviar

"Southerners still believe in beginning the New Year with a serving of black-eyed peas. The practice of eating them for luck dates back to the Civil War. Even though Sherman's troops either destroyed or stole most of the crops, they ignored the fields of black-eyed peas first planted to feed livestock, then fed to slaves, and then finally as a major food source for surviving Confederates. Served with greens (collards, mustard or turnip greens, or cabbage), the peas represent coins and the greens represent paper money. Texans believe the more you eat, the greater your luck.

"Texas caviar can be enjoyed as a salad or served with crackers and corn chips. For those who do not like black-eyed peas, look at the variation for a salad I make that people just adore and that looks beautiful in a glass or crystal serving dish." Linda

Ingredients

14 oz. can white corn, drained
14 oz. can black-eyed peas, drained
14 oz. can black beans, drained
2 bell peppers, diced
½ onion, diced
Vinaigrette or hot sauce dressing (recipes in Index)

Additions: chopped garlic, diced red peppers, and/or pinto beans (washed and drained)

Directions

1. Put all ingredients in large bowl and mix. **2.** Refrigerate for several hours before serving.

Variation

1. Begin with black beans, drained and rinsed. **2.** Add one can of drained corn. **3.** Add 1 tsp. garlic salt and ½ tsp. fresh black pepper. **4.** Pour on vinaigrette and let stand to absorb flavors. **5.** Add to that any of these possibilities: chopped grape tomatoes, any color pepper chopped, chopped black olives, and chopped cucumber. If you want to add protein, consider cheese cubes, chopped in half.

Tips for Tasty Appetizers

1. When served at a table as a first course, appetizers are often slightly larger in size and complement the entrée and dessert courses to follow.
2. The number of appetizers to serve varies depending on time of day of the gathering. If dinner follows, prepare 5–6 pieces per person. If it's a cocktail party or wedding, 10–12.
3. For a quick but impressive appetizer, spread green pepper, jalapeno or apricot jelly over cream cheese and serve with crackers.
4. Clean and peel celery sticks. Then fill with peanut butter or cream cheese. Sprinkle cream cheese with seasoning (Season All is a versatile brand to have on hand) and cut sticks on an angle for a pretty presentation.
5. French bread sliced on an angle and toasted makes a delicious base for various toppings; diced tomatoes and basil mixed together with olive oil and balsamic vinegar make a delicious bruschetta.
6. Put a slice of tomato on toasted bread. Sprinkle with garlic salt and pepper. Cover tomato with a slice of mozzarella cheese. Sprinkle with pepper and chopped basil. Heat until cheese is melted.
7. Melted cream cheese can be mixed with meat, fish, vegetables, and fruits for great dips. Replicate a Reuben sandwich by adding ¼ lb. sliced deli corned beef, chopped fine (about 1 cup) to 4 oz. (½ of 8 oz. pkg.) cream cheese, softened. Then add ½ cup Thousand Island dressing, ¾ cup well-drained sauerkraut, and 1 pkg. (8 oz.) Big Eye Swiss cheese slices, chopped. Bake for 20 minutes in 350° oven and serve with woven rye crackers like Triscuits.
8. Put potato chips, crackers or cereal on a cookie sheet and heat in the oven or under the broiler to freshen, but only for a few minutes. You do not want to brown them. Allow to cool, and then seal in a plastic bag or container.
9. Keep popcorn fresh and encourage more kernels to pop by storing in the freezer.
10. You can add almost anything to sour cream for a delicious dip. Mix in dill and chopped garlic, salt and pepper, and serve with vegetables. Add various soup mixes to sour cream, like leek or traditional onion, and serve with chips. Add diced vegetables to sour cream, your favorite seasonings, and herbs, and serve with crackers.

BREAD AND ROLLS

"There is nothing as aromatic as bread baking in the oven. It reminds us of all things good—family, holidays, and times gone by. Bread turns a simple meal into one that is truly memorable." Linda

Banana Bread

"No matter how hard my son tries to resist, he finally succumbs every time to this moist and flavorful recipe that I have been making since I was a teenager. Not only is it delicious alone or with cream cheese, but it is a great way to use up bananas that have turned brown (in fact, the browner the better). Serve right from the oven, and later store in foil wrap, that is if you have any left." Linda

Ingredients

5 or 6 bananas, very ripe
3 large eggs
1 stick of butter, melted
1 cup sugar
2 cups flour
1 tsp. baking soda

Additions: ¾ tsp. salt, ½ cup chopped walnuts

Directions

1. Oil and flour a loaf pan. **2.** Preheat oven to 350°. **3.** Mash bananas in a large mixing bowl. **4.** Add eggs and mix thoroughly. **5.** Mix in sugar, salt, butter, and baking soda. **6.** Add flour and mix thoroughly. **7.** Add nuts. **8.** Pour into pan and bake for 45 minutes or until brown.

Boston Brown Bread

"*Historically, brown bread was made from brown meal. Considered a less desirable grain product, it was inexpensive and often handed out to the poor, but when the health benefits of bran were discovered in 1865, the price often exceeded that of the finest flour.*

"*Boston or New England brown bread is a dark, slightly sweet bread cooked by steam in a can or cylindrical pan. It is traditionally served with New England baked beans because both require long hours of cooking. Leftovers freeze well. Cover and briefly microwave to refresh.*" Lael

Ingredients

2 cups corn meal
1 cup white flour
½ tsp. baking powder
1 cup buttermilk
½ cup molasses
Butter

Additions: 1 cup raisins and/or ¼ cup chopped walnuts. You might also substitute the more traditional flour used in this recipe. The best combination is ½ cup rye flour and ½ cup graham flour.

Directions

1. Mix dry ingredients with nuts and raisins, if desired. Then add liquids and mix well. **2.** Turn into buttered pan, a smooth-sided tin can, or a medium-sized oven-proof mixing bowl that will fit into steaming kettle or crockpot. Do not fill more than ⅔ full. Tightly cover container with heavy foil or a lid that fits tightly. **3.** Fill steaming pot or crockpot with water half way up the bread pan or dish. Do not fill so full it will boil over. **4.** Set bread container in steaming pot and cook tightly covered for 3 hours. **5.** Turn out of container and serve hot with butter or cream cheese.

Bran Muffins

"We've come to associate bran-anything with tactful advertisements about 'keeping regular,' so it's easy to forget that bran muffins also taste wonderful, especially when you add raisins." Lael

Ingredients
1 ¼ cup self-rising flour
½ cup sugar
2 cups all-bran cereal
1 ¼ cup milk
1 egg
¼ cup vegetable oil

Additions: 1 cup raisins added with milk and egg.

Directions
1. Mix flour and sugar. Set aside. **2.** Combine all-bran cereal and milk and let stand 2 minutes. Then add egg and oil and beat well. **3.** Add flour and mix well. **4.** Pour into non-stick muffin pan coated with oil or cooking spray. **5.** Bake at 400° for 20 minutes. Cool 10 minutes before serving.

Cream Biscuits

"I love biscuits, and I love to cheat when it comes to hard work in the kitchen. This recipe wins on both counts." Lael

Ingredients
2 cups self-rising flour   1 cup heavy whipping cream

Additions: 1–2 T. sugar, if you want to use for shortcake.

Directions
1. Preheat oven to 425°. **2.** Measure flour into a bowl and stir in cream. **3.** Turn dough onto a floured surface and knead 10 times. **4.** Roll to ¾" thickness and cut in rounds. **5.** Place on an ungreased baking sheet and cook for about 10 minutes or until lightly browned.

Buttermilk Biscuits

"In some parts of the country, especially the South, folks serve this recipe with sausage gravy as a meal in itself." Lael

Ingredients
2 T. vegetable oil
2 cups flour
3 tsp. baking powder
¼ tsp. baking soda
½ cup butter
¾ to 1 cup buttermilk

Additions: gravy, butter, honey, and/or jam.

Directions
1. Preheat oven to 425°. **2.** Spread vegetable oil in bottom of a baking pan. **3.** Stir together the dry ingredients. Cut in butter until it forms crumbs a bit smaller than peas. Stirring with a fork, add milk to make dough so moist that it is almost sticky. **4.** Turn dough onto floured surface and use floured palms and fingers to form it into a flat disk about 1½" thick. Using a cookie cutter or drinking glass, cut 2" biscuits, dipping cutter in flour before each cut. **5.** Bake 10–12 minutes until golden brown.

Cornbread

"Too often I've labored hard over a main course which garners only mild applause from dinner guests, who demolish my casually cooked cornbread and ask for the recipe.

I hate to admit that recipe is whatever is on the cornmeal box, which is usually the case because most cornmeal manufacturers know their product. However, for special occasions, I trot out this classic southern version of what is one of my favorite foods." Lael

Ingredients

⅔ cup self-rising flour
1⅓ cup yellow cornmeal
1 tsp. soda
2 eggs well beaten
1⅔ cup sour milk or buttermilk
¼ cup butter melted or cooking oil

Directions

1. Preheat oven to 350°. **2.** Combine dry ingredients. **3.** Combine liquids with butter or oil. **4.** Combine all ingredients and stir just enough to blend. Add vegetables, if desired. **5.** Turn into a greased 8½ x 11" pan. **6.** Pour in mixture and bake for 35–45 minutes.

Variation

Add 1 box frozen chopped broccoli, thawed, 1 small onion, chopped.

French Toast

"I'm still seeking a perfect French toast recipe that involves beaten egg whites to make it so light that it actually sort of floats on my plate. However, when camping, I often just mix up a couple of eggs, maybe with a dollop of milk, and plop a dot of butter in the pan for frying the soaked bread. Even done that simply, this favorite always tastes just wonderful in the wild and on the kitchen table." *Lael*

"French toast is my immediate go to when I have overnight company. It is easy, delicious, and so impressive when served sprinkled with powdered sugar. Just make sure you don't skimp on the butter. Your pan should sizzle when you put in the butter, and then it will brown your toast to perfection." *Linda*

Ingredients

Slices of whole wheat bread, cinnamon bread, raisin bread or stale French baguettes.
1 egg per two slices of bread
1 T. milk per two slices of bread
½ tsp. cinnamon per two slices of bread
Butter
Powdered sugar and/or maple syrup or praline sauce (recipe in Index).

Directions

1. Beat eggs with milk. **2.** Add cinnamon and mix again. **3.** Heat fry pan and add pats of butter to melt. **4.** Dip bread in mixture and put into fry pan. **5.** Cook until firm. Flip once. **6.** Sprinkle with sugar and/or serve with warmed syrup.

Variation

Spread with peanut or apple butter or with apple or apricot jam.

Fried Bread

"This has long been winter staple in New England, and it also became a Navajo favorite once flour was introduced to that culture. There is nothing better to appease a big appetite on a cold morning." Lael

Ingredients
White bread or wheat bread dough that has risen once

1 cup cooking oil

Additions: butter, honey, jam, and/or cinnamon and sugar

Directions
1. Heat oil in skillet. **2.** Flour dough just enough to keep it from sticking to your fingers, and shape it into flat, biscuit-sized pieces no thicker than ½". Drop each into hot oil. When oil side is brown, flip over and flatten uncooked side down hard into the oil with spatula or pancake flipper so the center will cook through as the down-side browns. **3.** Serve either hot or cold with the additions of your choice.

Hush Puppies

"Feeding your dog these little corn biscuits is an excellent way to keep it quiet, which is how this southern recipe supposedly got its name. And it has become a human favorite, too." Lael

Ingredients
1 cup corn meal
2 tsp. baking powder
½ cup water
1 ½ cups milk

1 large onion, finely diced
Oil enough for deep frying, about 1.5"

Additions: butter and 1 tsp. salt

Directions
1. Mix corn meal, baking powder and salt if desired. Add milk, water, and onion. **2.** If necessary, add more milk or meal to make dough workable so it sticks together. **3.** Form into pones (oblongs 5 x 3"). **4.** Deep fry in hot oil until brown. Drain and serve as is or with butter.

Spoon Bread

"I encountered this wonderful bread while living in the South and quickly made it a staple. As you can see from the recipe, it is a simple soufflé which costs practically nothing to make and dresses up any meal." Lael

Ingredients
2 cups milk
1 cup corn meal
3 T. butter

2 eggs (beat whites and yolks separately)
1 tsp. baking power

Directions
1. Preheat oven to 350°. **2.** Scald milk. **3.** Add meal and butter and stir until thick. **4.** Add beaten yolks and baking powder and set aside to cool. **5.** Just before spooning into buttered pan, fold in stiffly beaten egg whites. **6.** Bake at once for 30 minutes.

No Knead Bread

"This super-simple bread far surpasses in flavor that of much more complicated recipes. It was a favorite with a multinational group of charter boat wives who cooked in tiny galleys when I sailed in the Virgin Islands during the early 1960s, and I still prefer it, even when enjoying the use of a big kitchen. I also use the recipe for quick and easy pizza dough and cinnamon rolls." Lael

Ingredients
1½ cups lukewarm water
1 T. sugar
1 T. dry yeast
4 cups flour

Additions: butter or shortening to grease baking tins if you don't use nonstick. You might also want to butter the bowl in which the dough will rise.

Directions
1. Combine water, yeast, and sugar in a large bowl. Let stand about five minutes until yeast dissolves. **2.** Stir in flour, gradually, kneading the last of it with your hands. Leave dough in the bowl or place in another mixing bowl that has been greased, and cover with damp towel. Set in warm spot and let rise about one hour, until double its bulk. **3.** Toss on a floured surface and knead lightly. Place in two bread tins and let rise about one hour until double bulk, preheating oven to 400° so it will be ready. **4.** Bake 45 minutes or until a golden brown. Turn bread out of tins as soon as it comes out of the oven. If you want to cut it while it is hot, use a serrated knife.

Popovers

"Specially designed popover pans or oven-proof custard cups are needed for this recipe. If you use conventional muffin tins, the popovers may not rise sufficiently to rate their name. When I'm desperate enough to use muffin tins, I call the results, 'Popunders.' They won't look too impressive, but they still taste good." Lael

Ingredients
3 eggs
1 cup flour
1 cup milk
3 T. oil or melted butter

Nonstick baking spray if you use nonstick tins or custard cups instead of the traditionally seasoned cast iron popover pans.

Additions: butter, honey, and/or jam.

Directions
1. Pre-heat oven to 375°. Heat popover pan. **2.** Except spray, combine all other ingredients in a blender. Beat at high speed for about four minutes. **3.** Pour into popover pans or custard cups sprayed with nonstick coating, filling cups a bit over half full. Bake for 45 minutes. Do not open oven door for the first 20 minutes.

Refrigerator Rolls

"This simple recipe can also be used for cinnamon rolls. It makes an excellent pizza crust, too. The good news is that it can be prepared in advance and keeps up to 24 hours in the refrigerator, if you place it in a bowl where it has room to rise, and keep it covered with a damp towel." Lael

Ingredients

2 T. dry yeast
2 cups lukewarm water
½ cup sugar
1 egg
¼ cup melted shortening or cooking oil
6½–7 cups flour

Additions: Butter or shortening to grease baking tin, if you don't use nonstick spray. You might also want to butter the bowl in which the dough will rise. The basic recipe works for pizza dough as is.

If you want to make cinnamon rolls, you will need to prepare a filling of 1 cup sugar, 3 tsp. cinnamon, ½ cup chopped nuts and ½ cup raisins. To make the filling stick, you will also need ½ cup melted butter.

Directions

1. Combine water, yeast, and sugar in a large bowl and let stand for five minutes until yeast dissolves. Beat in eggs and oil. **2.** Stir and gradually add half the flour. Stir vigorously for about two minutes and then work in the rest of the flour. (Toward the end, you may want to knead it with your hands. You can do that right in the bowl). **3.** Leave in the bowl or place in another mixing bowl that has been greased, and cover with damp cloth. Place in refrigerator until you want to use it, punching down occasionally if it rises. **4.** Then, form into rolls. **5.** Place rolls on a greased cookie sheet about an inch apart and cover with damp cloth. Let them rise in a warm place until double bulk. **6.** Preheat oven to 375° while you are letting the rolls rise (Rising will take about a half hour in a warm room.). **7.** Bake 12–15 minutes until brown.

Resurrection Rolls or Magic Puffs

"This recipe, which came from my dear friend Barb, will astound you and delight your guests, particularly the young ones. The marshmallow melts and disappears, of course, and combines with the cinnamon and butter to make a unique treat. This is a great cooking project to do with kids who will love to eat the fruits of their labor and will remember fondly their time with you in the kitchen." Linda

Ingredients
8 oz. tube crescent rolls
1 bag giant marshmallows
½ cup butter, melted
1 tsp. cinnamon
½ cup sugar

Directions
1. Preheat oven to 350°. **2.** Combine cinnamon and sugar in a bowl. **3.** Roll one marshmallow in warm butter. Then roll it in sugar mixture and place on one crescent roll triangle. **4.** Wrap marshmallow with pastry, being sure all edges are pinched tightly. **5.** Roll each crescent roll round in butter and put into a muffin pan. **6.** Bake for 10–12 minutes.

Sourdough Pancakes

"Before you begin sourdough cooking, you need a cup or so of sourdough starter. Some people are proud to brag they got their first starter from a batch handed down through several generations of pioneers. However, if you consider all the things that could have fallen into a stash of ancient starter over those many years, you may not want to go that route. Some people purchase expensive "starter kits" for which the basic production cost was probably well under a dollar. I recommend creating your own (also under a dollar)." Lael

Ingredients
2 cups sourdough starter
2 T. sugar
1 tsp. baking soda
2 egg yolks, beaten stiff
⅔ cup evaporated milk

Directions
1. Mix sugar and soda and fold gently into sourdough just before you are ready to cook. **2.** Mix in milk. **3.** Fold in beaten egg yolks. **4.** Cook on a griddle or in a frying pan as you would regular pancake mix. Traditional sourdoughs are the size of silver dollars, but you can make them larger if you like. Cook in oil or in a Teflon skillet.

Variation
For **Sourdough Waffles,** just add 3 T. of oil to the recipe.

Sourdough Starter

Ingredients
1 package dry yeast (1 T)
1 cup lukewarm water
2 cups white flour (or more)

Directions
1. In the evening, dissolve yeast in water and stir in 1 cup flour. This mixture should have the consistency of heavy cream and will fall off the spoon in large drops. If it is too thick (not all flour works the same way), add more lukewarm water to gain cream consistency. **2.** Put in 2-quart plastic, glass or crockery container that has a screw-on cover. Set cover aside and top with a clean towel, so the mixture can "breathe" and grow. **3.** Allow the mixture to sit untouched for two more days. **4.** The night before using, mix in 1 or 2 cups of flour and about ⅔ cup lukewarm water per cup. Leave covered with a towel at room temperature overnight. Mixture will work and rise. **5.** In the morning, move starter to a large mixing bowl. Wash sourdough pot and return at least one cup of virgin starter to it. Cover it tightly and store in the refrigerator for later use. What's left, you can use for other recipes.

Tips for Better Bread

1. If bananas have darkened, peel, smash, and freeze them. Add to breads, cakes or smoothies.
2. One way to preserve the flavor of fresh herbs is to make herb butter. Let the butter soften and then mix in finely chopped herbs. The butter freezes well, and you can serve it spread on bread or with seafood or chicken.
3. Successful bread dough is all about the ratio of flour to water. You will get more consistent and reliable results if you carefully measure the flour and liquid. One half the weight of the flour is the amount of water you'll need. Even if you think the dough seems too sticky, if your ratio is correct, your bread will be fine. Resist adding extra flour. It invariably leads to a dense loaf that does not rise as much as it should.
4. If you're using a bread recipe that calls for putting all your ingredients, including the yeast, together in the mixer, warm up the water called for in the recipe so the yeast will do its job. Add a pinch of sugar to ensure the yeast eats. If, after stirring, you do not have bubbles, your yeast is dead, and you will have to add more.
5. To avoid an air pocket under the crust, slash the dough once lengthwise for a sandwich loaf and several times on an angle for a baguette loaf.
6. To freeze fresh bread, make sure it is completely cooled first. Put the bread in one freezer bag, remove air and then place it in a second, and remove air. Will keep beautifully for months. It will keep even more beautifully if you don't slice it first.
7. You can slice the bread partially frozen, so that you can get thinner, more even slices.
8. Make sandwiches on frozen bread. The bread will be thawed by the time you're ready to eat. You can also toast the bread while frozen.
9. To keep bread fresh longer, put a rib of celery in your bread bag.
10. Use organic flour that is stone ground for the best bread free of two rounds of pesticides and chemical bleaching.

SALADS

"Hearty spinach leaves or delicate lettuce (Romaine, red leaf, Bibb lettuce, butter, or iceberg) that almost melts on the tongue, tangy tomatoes, crisp celery, and cucumbers are just a few of the vegetables that you can use to create a salad that is not only healthy but beautiful as well.

"Add crunch with croutons, pita chips, nuts and/or seeds, and variety by combining vegetables and fruits including berries, apples, grapes and/or mandarin oranges.

"Add beans, chopped chicken or beef, and/or hard-boiled eggs, and you've even taken care of your required protein in delicious fashion. There is no question anymore that if you replace large portions of protein with large portions of salad instead, you will be leaner and healthier." Linda

Artichoke and Lima Beans

"When provisioning to sail around the world in a small boat, I purchased a case of canned lima beans because I knew they had more vitamins and staying power than practically any other vegetable. Shortly thereafter, a seasoned sailor signed aboard to help us learn the ropes. Because he was a good friend for whom I'd cooked before, I was surprised to learn he hated lima beans which had become a large part of my menus.

"'But they have lots of vitamins, Dusty!' I pleaded.

"'Great,' he replied. 'I'll take one with a glass of water.'

"For that reason, I've never again served to company anything involving lima beans. Linda's recipe featuring artichokes might make a difference. It's as glamorous as it is nutritious." Lael

"I learned this delicious recipe from my husband's grandmother. She was a good cook but a master with layered dough dishes that oozed with the delicious cheeses she sold in the small corner store that she and her husband ran in Philadelphia." Linda

Ingredients

½ cup olive oil
2 T. lemon juice
2 T. fresh dill, chopped or dried dill
1 onion, diced

1 bag frozen baby lima beans, thawed and drained
1 jar artichoke hearts, drained and cut in half

Additions: 1 tsp. salt, ½ tsp. pepper

Directions

1. Cook frozen lima beans in salted water. Reserve ⅛ cup to add to salad. **2.** Sauté onion in 1 T. olive oil. **3.** Add artichokes to drained lima beans and mix with sautéed onions. **4.** Add water, lemon juice, remaining olive oil and dill, and mix well. **5.** Refrigerate overnight.

Variation

Add 2 T. balsamic vinegar to the dressing.

Bean Salad

"I got this recipe from my Aunt Mimi, who was really more like a big sister to me than an aunt. Before she married my Uncle Chuck, she and I shared her bedroom whenever I went to visit my grandparents, which was as often as I could. I still remember the smell of her nail polish and the brightly colored bottles of perfume that lined her dresser.

"As a little girl, I was intrigued by all her primping for work, and then as a young married woman, I was her most avid student in the kitchen as she made cheese from scratch, tabouli (a grain and parsley salad) and creative concoctions that combined beautifully vegetables and fruit." Linda

Ingredients

16 oz. can each of green, kidney and cannellini beans
1 cup green pepper, diced
4 T. onion, diced
Sweet vinaigrette dressing (recipe in Index)

Additions: 1 tsp. salt, 1 tsp. pepper, 1 pinch basil, yellow beans, canned corn

Directions

1. Drain all beans and put into a serving bowl. **2.** Add green pepper and onion and mix. **3.** Mix other ingredients for the dressing and pour over beans. **4.** Cover and chill overnight.

Caesar Salad

"I didn't encounter Caesar salad until I moved to California in the 1970s and discovered I could eat it happily at least six nights a week. Although it had become popular there in the 1920s, it took me six months to find a recipe that produced the results I was enjoying in expensive restaurants.

"But a note of caution! Later I worked in western British Columbia and Yukon Territory where Caesar salad served in most Canadian restaurants included all sorts of leftovers from the previous day's menu. To avoid it, I mostly stuck with a chain called American Pizza which boasted a new-fangled invention called the 'salad bar.'

"My Caesar formula is classic, and I beg you to take good care of this knowledge." Lael

Ingredients

½ cup olive oil
3 tsp. vinegar
1 lemon, juiced

1 fresh egg
1 head romaine lettuce
¼ cup grated Parmesan cheese

Additions: 1 clove or more of minced garlic, dash of anchovy paste or whole anchovies, bread croutons, cooked chicken or shrimp.

Directions

1. Tear up head of romaine and place in big salad bowl. **2.** Beat egg and add oil, vinegar and lemon juice, plus garlic and anchovy paste if you decide to add them. Pour over lettuce and toss with Parmesan and croutons if desired. **3.** Add toppings such as anchovies or chicken for extras, and serve super cold.

Cole Slaw

"Maine winters were often worse than those in central Alaska and fresh vegetables were a rarity when I was growing up. Luckily, cabbage, carrots, and onions would keep long enough to provide basic staples until our garden could kick in again. My first kitchen responsibility—assigned when I finally got tall enough to peer into the sink—was to make cole slaw, and I still treasure the battered wooden bowl and chopper with which I preformed that duty. My recipe varies a bit from the one to which my mother sentenced me, but it's hard to argue with the basics." Lael

Ingredients

4 cups cabbage, cored and shredded or chopped fine
1 small onion, chopped
¼ cup sugar
3 T. white wine vinegar
2 tsp. prepared horseradish
½ tsp. ground mustard (or ½ tsp. regular mustard)

Additions: ¾ cup slivered carrots, ½ small green pepper, finely chopped and/or ¼ tsp. celery seed.

Directions

1. Mix cabbage and onion. Add carrots and green pepper if desired. **2.** In a small container with tight fitting lid, combine the sugar, vinegar, horseradish, and mustard for dressing. Close lid and shake to combine. **3.** Mix dressing with vegetables and refrigerate for about an hour before serving, if you have time.

Variation (on dressing)
Ingredients

2 cups mayonnaise
¼ cup sugar
¼ cup vinegar
2 tsp. salt
2 tsp. celery seed (optional)
4 tsp. prepared mustard (optional)

Cranberry and Pineapple Frozen Salad

"This is my daughter, Tricia's, favorite accompaniment to turkey dinner, so not only did I make it at home for each holiday celebration, but if she was hosting, I would even pull it out of the freezer and cart it to wherever she was living at the time. I promise your guests will always ask for seconds." Linda

Ingredients

8 oz. pkg. cream cheese, softened
½ cup mayonnaise
½ cup sugar
20 oz. can whole cranberry sauce
20 oz. can crushed pineapple with juice
16 oz. container of whipped topping, thawed

Additions: add ½ cup chopped walnuts to the mixture before freezing.

Directions

1. Mix cream cheese and sugar until smooth. Then mix in mayonnaise until smooth. **2.** Add fruits. **3.** Fold in whipped topping. **4.** Freeze overnight in a pretty mold. **5.** Serve frozen, cut in slices.

Greek Salad

"The key to this dish is fresh, juicy tomatoes, good olives and olive oil. These ingredients not only contribute to a flavorful salad, but the dressing makes a wonderful dipping sauce for bread."

Linda

Ingredients

2 tomatoes, peeled (optional) and chopped
½ onion, any color, cut in half and finely sliced
¼ cup olives (Kalamata is a good type)
2 oz. feta cheese
3 T. olive oil
¼ tsp. oregano, fresh is best

Additions: sliced green/red peppers, chopped cucumbers and fresh parsley, fresh garlic or garlic salt, 1 T. lemon juice or 1 T. vinegar

Directions

1. Put tomatoes in a bowl. **2.** Add onion (and the additional vegetables suggested). **3.** Pour on olive oil and mix. **4.** Sprinkle on oregano. **5.** Add olives. **6.** Add feta cheese either in one chunk on top or in bits mixed in. **7.** Mix and serve.

Fruit Salad

"This is quick, beautiful, delicious, and healthy. Add as much or as little of the ingredients as you'd like for yourself or need for your company." *Linda*

Ingredients

Red grapes, sliced in half
Banana, sliced
Strawberries, sliced
Blueberries
Walnuts or pecans, chopped
Vanilla yogurt

Directions

1. Mix fruits in bowl. **2.** Add nuts. **3.** Mix in yogurt and serve cold.

Macaroni and Tuna Fish

"When we were young, my mom was a "work at home" wife, so money was tight and she had to be careful with the food budget. She got creative with more inexpensive proteins. This creamy dish was one result, and whenever I make it, I think of my mom. You can serve this right after you make it or you can refrigerate it. Warm or chilled, it is delicious." Linda

Ingredients

1 box elbow or tri-color macaroni
2 cans of tuna fish, drained
1 onion, diced

1 cup mayonnaise or Miracle Whip
1 tsp. black pepper
2 tsp. garlic salt

Directions

1. Boil macaroni (The trick to making more flavorful pasta that doesn't come out sticky is to add salt and a little vegetable oil to the boiling water before adding the pasta.). **2.** Drain macaroni and put into a large bowl. **3.** Add tuna fish and onion and mix well. **4.** Mix mayonnaise with spices and add to pasta and tuna and mix well.

Mandarin Orange Salad

"I usually keep a can or two of mandarin oranges in my refrigerator to snack on or to use for the recipe that follows. It is elegant enough to serve unexpected dinner guests with very little effort." Lael

Ingredients
1 small head romaine lettuce
8 oz. can mandarin oranges, drained
¼ cup sugar
¼ cup balsamic vinegar
1 cup sweetened pecans or walnuts, whole
½ cup oil

Additions: chopped cucumbers, chopped red bell pepper and/or sliced carrots.

Directions
1. Combine sugar, oil and vinegar for salad dressing. **2.** Wash, dry and break lettuce into bite size pieces. **3.** Add oranges (and other suggested vegetables) and sweetened nuts. **4.** Pour on dressing and toss.

Oriental Salad

"This salad lends itself to many variations with a variety of dressings. The recipe that follows is Linda's. My version includes toasted sesame seeds and a sauce of honey, soy sauce, and vegetable oil (2 tablespoons each)." Lael

Ingredients

- 16 oz. pkg. of broccoli slaw or broccoli stems peeled and julienned into 1" strips
- 2 pkgs. Ramen noodle soup, chicken flavored
- 1 cup honey roasted peanuts
- 1 cup Craisins (cranberries in raisin form)
- 1 bunch green onions, chopped fine
- Sweet Vinaigrette (recipe in Index) mixed with 1½ pkg. chicken stock from Ramen soup mix.

Additions: 1 red bell pepper, chopped fine

Directions

1. Mix sweet vinaigrette with chicken stock from soup mix.
2. Add dressing to the vegetables and refrigerate in a plastic bag for about 4 hours.
3. Add noodles, broken into bits, and peanuts to mix just before serving.

Pasta Salad

"This recipe is also perfect for left-over pasta that you have not yet doused with sauce. In fact, this salad is so good, I always cook more pasta than I need for the hot dish I am preparing and refrigerate the rest. It can stay for several days, but before tossing it with the others ingredients, rinse pasta first in slightly warm water to refresh." Linda

Ingredients

1 box of pasta—bow tie, tri-color, or spirals
1 onion, diced
Cherry tomatoes, halved
Green olives or black olives
Cheddar cheese, cut in cubes
Vinaigrette, savory
 (recipe in Index)

Additions: salt, garlic salt, fresh basil or dill, cucumbers, chopped bell peppers

Directions

1. Boil pasta in salted water with a little oil. **2.** Drain pasta and put in a glass bowl. **3.** Add remainder of ingredients, mix, and serve cold.

Pea Pod Imperial

"The Boston lettuce alone sold me on this classic, even though it is usually as expensive as it is delicious. Adding frozen pea pods with or without chestnuts is akin to eating lamb chops without the serious guilt. Yes, it makes me feel like I am a rich Mandarin." Lael

Ingredients

2, 10 oz. pkgs. frozen pea pods with water chestnuts
2 cloves garlic, minced
4 T. lemon juice
4 T. vegetable oil
4 T. sesame seeds, roasted
1 head Boston lettuce

Additions: 1½ tsp. salt and ½ tsp. fresh ground pepper

Directions

1. Cook pods and chestnuts according to directions and chill. **2.** Line salad bowl with lettuce and fill with pods and chestnuts. **3.** Blend oil, garlic and lemon juice. Add salt and pepper, if desired, and pour on salad. **4.** Sprinkle sesame seeds on top and serve immediately.

Waldorf Salad

"This classic was created in the late 1890s by Oscar Tschirky, the chef of the famous Waldorf Hotel in New York City. His recipe did not originally contain walnuts, but they are a perfect addition. So are green grapes if you happen to have some handy." Lael

Ingredients

3 cups unpeeled apples, cored and diced
1 cup celery, chopped
¼ cup walnuts, chopped
1 T. lemon juice
Mayonnaise to taste
Lettuce leaves

Directions

1. Sprinkle apples with lemon juice to keep them from turning brown. **2.** Add celery and walnuts and enough mayonnaise to moisten. **3.** Toss lightly and serve on lettuce leaves.

Potato Salad

"Gourmets will tell you there are mashing potatoes and baking potatoes and have you running every which way to find the right ones for each task. But any brand of potatoes should work as long as they are not overcooked. Prepare at least 6 hours in advance if you can, and it's even better the second day." Lael

"My mother made the best potato salad. She chopped the potatoes small, added chopped, hard-boiled eggs and diced onions and celery. Her dressing was simple—¼ cup apple cider vinegar mixed with the 2 cups mayonnaise. Add salt and pepper, and you won't be able to stop eating the stuff." Linda

Ingredients

6 large potatoes, chopped in small cubes
3 dill pickle slices, diced
1 small green pepper, diced
3 celery stalks, diced
¼ medium onion, diced
2 cups mayonnaise

Additions: ½ tsp. prepared mustard, 1 minced clove garlic and/or 2 green onions cut in small pieces and a couple of hard boiled eggs cut in sections.

Directions

1. Boil potatoes, peel and cut into 1" squares. Refrigerate. **2.** Mix other ingredients. Add potatoes, plus mustard and garlic if desired. **3.** Place on bed of lettuce; garnish with sliced eggs.

Note: Keeps well for a day or two in refrigerator. Don't keep it much longer than that, however, because you can't trust mayonnaise or chopped onion.

Spinach Salad with Fruit

"Fresh spinach will generally outlast thin-leafed lettuce in your refrigerator vegetable drawer, and it will also stand you in better stead if a long afternoon of work lies ahead." *Lael*

"Where once I used spinach only occasionally, now I use lettuce only occasionally. I have made the switch entirely from using lettuce to using spinach in almost all my salads. It has far more nutrients than lettuce and a bolder taste." *Linda*

Ingredients
9 oz. bag fresh spinach
1 cup apples, unpeeled and chopped
½ cup raisins or Craisins (dried cranberries)
½ cup slivered almonds
½ red onion, sliced in rounds
Sweet vinaigrette (recipe in Index)

Directions
1. Mix all ingredients. 2. Mix dressing and pour on just before serving.

Variations
Add sliced strawberries and/or grapes, pecans, carrots, or substitute with vegetables including cucumbers, cherry tomatoes, chopped peppers of any color, Great Northern beans, cubed chicken or ham, and savory vinaigrette (recipe in Index).

Tomato Salad Italian

"It is best to prepare this dish about two hours ahead of use and refrigerate." Linda

Ingredients
4 ripe tomatoes, sliced in thin rounds
2 T. basil, chopped, plus sprigs for garnish
½ cup olive oil
2½ T. balsamic vinegar
1 clove garlic minced
6 oz. fresh mozzarella cheese, sliced in small rounds

Directions
1. Mix oil, garlic, and vinegar and let stand at room temperature. **2.** Arrange tomatoes on platter and top evenly with chopped basil. **3.** Spoon oil and vinegar mixture over tomatoes (reserve some to dress the cheese), cover, and let marinate in refrigerator an hour or two, if possible. **4.** Serve topped with cheese slices that have been topped with a little dressing and small sprigs of basil.

Variations
1. For Bruschetta, dice tomatoes, mince garlic and basil, then mix with olive oil, balsamic vinegar and salt and pepper. Pile onto thinly sliced Italian bread that has been toasted and spread with butter and sprinkled with Parmesan cheese.

2. For Antipasto: Chop in half cherry tomatoes and add Greek or black olives, mozzarella balls, salami or prosciutto, chopped chives and fresh oregano. Dress with oil and balsamic vinegar in the amounts above and layer beautifully on a bed of lettuce.

Salad Dressings

Bleu Cheese

"I'd never heard of bleu cheese when I left rural Maine. I had heard about Roquefort and wondered who would want to eat cheese so rotten that it could crawl off your cracker? But having established that bleu cheese at least sat still, I gingerly tried it and was immediately charmed. In that era, however, there were few bottled dressings on the market, and I never did find a recipe for bleu cheese dressing. Finally, after enjoying it at a number of progressive restaurants, I developed my own formula (without preservatives and a ton of sodium), which still stands me in good stead." Lael

Ingredients
¼ cup milk
3 cups mayonnaise
1 cup sour cream
2 tsp. garlic salt
4 oz. crumbled bleu cheese
  or more

Directions
1. Put the milk, mayonnaise, sour cream, bleu cheese and garlic salt in a blender. Cover and process until smooth. **2.** Refrigerate until serving. If you want it chunky, blend all ingredients but the cheese; then add cheese and mix to desired consistency.

Creamy Italian

"I once lived in a grand Italian villa overlooking Lake Como. The chef was justifiably proud of the rich oil that he had pressed from the estate's olive trees and served a dressing of olive oil, vinegar and salt on the lettuce alone salad that was included in his grandly formal nightly dinners. I loved the combination but after a month of nothing but, I found this Creamy Italian a welcome change." Lael

Ingredients
¼ cup mayonnaise
3 T. red wine vinegar
2 T. sour cream
2 T. olive oil
1 tsp. Italian seasoning
1 garlic clove, minced

Directions
1. Mix ingredients in a blender. 2. Add salt and pepper to taste.

Mustard Dressing

"Almost any commercial mustard will work for this recipe, but Dijon mustard has special flavor. The condiment is named for the town of Dijon, France, where manufacturers perfected the art of blending ground brown mustard seeds with secret combinations of other spices and alcohol." Lael

Ingredients
3 T. Dijon mustard
3 T. champagne vinegar
½ cup olive oil
½ tsp. kosher salt
¼ tsp. pepper

Directions
1. Whisk mustard and vinegar together. 2. Add spices.
3. Gradually whisk in olive oil.

Variation
For Honey Mustard, mix ¾ cup mayonnaise, 2 T. mustard, Dijon preferred, and ¼ cup honey.

Traditional French Dressing

"This was the first 'store bought' salad dressing I ever encountered after coming to think all there was out there was the mayonnaise I'd learned to spark up a bit for my mother's stand-by cole slaw recipe. As a country girl, I decided this 'new' combination from France was quite sophisticated, and so was I for having the courage to speak right up and order it at restaurants. Those were definitely simpler days, and I'm grateful for the innocent joy they gave me while discovering a new world of taste." Lael

Ingredients
1½ cups vegetable oil
½ cup vinegar
1 cup ketchup
¾ cup sugar
1 tsp. lemon juice
1 tsp. paprika

Directions
1. Put ingredients in a blender and puree. **2.** Cover and refrigerate. **3.** Add salt and pepper to taste.

Vinaigrette French Dressing

Ingredients
3 T. extra virgin olive oil
1 T. balsamic vinegar
2 T. Dijon mustard
Salt and pepper

Directions
1. Add Dijon mustard to oil and mix thoroughly. **2.** Add salt and pepper. **3.** Add vinegar and mix thoroughly until dressing is thickened.

Ranch Dressing

"This is traditional Ranch Dressing only with fewer calories. For those of us trying to pack on some pounds, mayonnaise and whole milk are, of course, the answer." Lael

"The first time I ate traditional ranch dressing was in New Jersey at my friend Judy's house in 1973. I remember it so precisely because I thought it was the most delicious dressing I had ever tasted, and look all these years later, ranch dressing is served everywhere, even in the most elegant restaurants." Linda

Ingredients
1 cup Greek yogurt, plain
½ cup 1% milk
1 pkg. Hidden Valley Ranch Dressing

Directions
1. Mix ingredients. **2.** Refrigerate for at least one hour before serving on salads or baked potatoes.

Russian Dressing

"Despite its name, this recipe is an all-American invention. Some historians attribute it to James E. Colburn of Nashua, New Hampshire. We do know Colburn originally called his version 'Russian Mayonnaise,' perhaps because he experimented with adding a dash of caviar to make it even more exciting." Lael

"I learned this simple version in my Home Economics class at Montgomery Hills Junior High School. It is so good, though, that I still make up a batch whenever I make hamburgers, BLTs and Reuben sandwiches." Linda

Ingredients
½ cup mayonnaise
2 T. ketchup
½ tsp. coarse salt
¼ tsp. fresh pepper

Directions
1. Whisk ingredients together until all lumps are gone and it is pink in color. **2.** Refrigerate and serve cold.

Sweet and Savory Vinaigrette

"This basic dressing is extremely versatile. If you make it with garlic salt and spices, it is delicious on any salad with any vegetables, beans, chopped meats, poultry or combination thereof. Make the sweet version for salads to which you add fruit." Linda

Ingredients

⅔ cup olive oil

1 T. sugar or equivalent sugar substitute to make the sweet vinaigrette

⅓ cup balsamic vinegar

1 T. Lawry's Garlic Salt to make the savory vinaigrette

Additions: 1 tsp. basil, 1 tsp. dill, 1 tsp. oregano, 1 tsp. thyme, or 1 tsp. celery flakes, depending on the flavor you'd like.

Directions

1. Combine ingredients and allow an hour before pouring so flavors will blend. **2.** If you have refrigerated what is left over, be sure to take it out so olive oil will "warm up" before pouring on.

Thousand Island Dressing

"The strange name apparently honors a clever cook who lived on one of the thousand islands in the St. Lawrence River between the United States and Canada. Or perhaps it refers to the dots of sweet pickle relish suspended in its mayonnaise base. Whatever its origin, why purchase this rich treat at a store when this easy recipe is not only delicious but preservative-free?" Lael

Ingredients

½ cup mayonnaise

2 tsp. sweet pickle relish

1 T. vinegar

2 T. ketchup

2 tsp. sugar

1 tsp. finely chopped onion

Directions

1. Combine all ingredients and stir well. **2.** Refrigerate in a covered container for at least two hours, stirring occasionally so that the flavors blend and the sugar dissolves properly.

Sweetened Mayonnaise Dressing

"Salads can be really beautiful and layering them in a trifle or glass bowl can show them off well. Begin with a layer of red-leaf lettuce, then cover that with slices of any kind of tomato, then add a layer of spinach leaves, then shredded carrots, then slices of cucumber, then hard-boiled eggs, then baby peas, then your favorite nuts and/or seeds.

"Cover the top layer with the dressing below, sprinkle on paprika, and garnish with anything green. Serve it at the table to lots of praise. If you want to make this early in the morning, cover the top layer with a wet paper towel and refrigerate. Add dressing right before serving." *Linda*

Ingredients
¼ tsp. pepper
various vegetables
1 cup mayonnaise or Miracle Whip
1 pkg. artificial sweetener (or to taste)
Paprika

Directions
1. Follow directions above for assembling vegetables. **2.** Mix the dressing and refrigerate.

Tips for Special Salads

1. To refresh frozen vegetables and fruits, pour hot water over them to rinse off frozen-water taste.

2. We use the word "cooking" vegetables reservedly. Steam your vegetables for the best flavor and greatest intake of vitamins and minerals. Put as little water as possible in the pan, cover tightly, and cook just until the vegetables become brightly colored. Drain immediately. Save the cooking water to add to other pots of food, gravies, or soups. You will be making good use of the vitamins and minerals that have been deposited in that water.

3. To reduce the amount of butter you put on vegetables before serving, add a teaspoon to the cooking water first for flavor infusion, or cook the vegetables in chicken or beef broth instead for even fewer calories. You might also consider buying an oil spritzer which flavors beautifully without drenching the food.

4. Bake thinly sliced vegetables that have been spritzed with olive oil and favorite seasonings including garlic, sea or seasoned salt, and black or cayenne pepper. Kale, zucchini, and potato lend themselves perfectly to this process.

5. The best way to store fresh celery is to wrap it in aluminum foil and put it in the refrigerator. It will keep for weeks.

6. Keep garlic cloves in the freezer. Peel and chop them before thawing. To prevent garlic from drying out in the refrigerator, store in oil. When you've used all the garlic, add the oil to vinegar and use as salad dressing.

7. It is recommended that ground spices be replaced every six months unless kept in the refrigerator. Spices do lose strength over time and can become rancid if you do not keep them in a dry, cool place, so taste-test your dishes for potency. Do not store them over your stove where steam can ruin them. Unless you know you will use them up fairly quickly, buy a bottle with a friend and split the contents.

8. Hold fresh herbs together in a small bunch and snip with kitchen scissors. The herbs will be light and fluffy, not wet and wilted as they often get when chopped.

9. Lettuce and spinach keep better if you store them in the refrigerator without washing first. Wash the leaves carefully to remove dirt and pesticides the day you are going to use them. Use leaves in salads and for wrapping foods instead of bread. Vegetable wraps are delicious and lower in calories.

SOUPS, STEWS, AND CHOWDERS

"Any recipe here will provide a nice beginning for formal meals or meals with several courses, but it might also be considered a meal in itself when you add a salad and dessert. If you're surprised by company and/or find yourself with a low budget, serve with homemade bread, rolls, popovers, or top with dumplings. You'll not only look like a great host, but you might be classed as a gourmet." Lael

Beef Stew

"This recipe freezes beautifully, and I'm not secure during a northern winter if I don't have a container or two of this recipe in storage for shivering emergencies. I know chicken soup is supposed to cure ills, but for me, beef stew is the best backup. I like the canned kind, too, but my own version has no sodium to worry about. Instead, there is the encouraging hint of red wine that would never work in chicken soup." Lael

Ingredients

1 ½ lb. boneless stew beef, chopped into cubes
2 T. flour
1 T. oil
½ cup onion, chopped
2 ½ cups water, chicken, beef or vegetable broth
2 cups raw, peeled potatoes cut in 1" cubes

Additions: 1 cup sliced carrots, ½ cup sliced mushrooms, 2 cups canned tomatoes, 1 minced clove garlic, 1 bay leaf, 1 tsp. thyme leaves. You might also consider substituting ½ cup red wine for the same amount of water or beef broth.

Directions

1. Dredge beef in flour and brown in oil in large skillet. **2.** Add onion and garlic, if desired, and cook until onion is tender. **3.** Stir in water and seasonings. (If you plan to use wine, stir in just 2 cups of water or broth at this point). Simmer covered one hour. **4.** Add potatoes with carrots, tomatoes, mushrooms, and/or wine if desired. **5.** Cook another 30 minutes and serve.

Borscht

"On a rough visit to Moscow in mid-winter before the Iron Curtain came down, I found myself trailed by the KGB and then briefly arrested. Otherwise, I thoroughly enjoyed the trip. Though my budget was limited, times were even tougher for my Russian peers. But along with the warmth of new friendships, I discovered borscht in all its infinite varieties. It was always superb... especially when enjoyed with a capitalistic glass of champagne." Lael

Ingredients

1 2/3 cups canned beets with their juice or beet baby food
1 cup chicken or vegetable broth
1 cup cabbage, shredded
1/2 tsp. lemon juice
1 T. minced onion
1/2 cup sour cream

Additions: leftover meat, including beef or lamb, chopped into small pieces.

Directions

1. Puree beets in a blender or just chop as fine as you can get them.
2. Put beets, their juice, broth, cabbage, and onion in kettle and bring to a boil. (Add meat if desired.) Simmer 5 minutes. Then stir in lemon juice. 3. Serve hot or chilled. In either case, sour cream is a great topping.

Chicken Noodle Soup

"*Drinking chicken soup to help cure a cold is not just an old wives' tale. There are properties in the broth that can actually help those who are ill, so drink up. If this recipe is too much to serve and use later for leftovers, cut the chicken in half and freeze one half. Then cut the other ingredients in half as well and prepare as directed, or you can prepare as directed and freeze beautifully what you can't eat.*" Linda

Ingredients

1 whole chicken with its skin
1 gallon water and 6 bouillon cubes or ½ gallon water and ½ gallon chicken broth
5 celery stalks, chopped
1 large white onion, chopped
3 T. vegetable soup seasoning
2 cups noodles (wide noodles are particularly good)

Additions: 1 cup carrots, string beans or peas, 2 T. garlic salt, pepper.

Directions

1. Add all ingredients except noodles to a soup pot. Boil the chicken until meat falls off the bone. **2.** Take chicken out and cool. Remove all chicken from bone, chop into small cubes and return to soup pot. **3.** This makes more soup than some would care to deal with. If that is your case, save part of the broth and meat to use in other recipes. **4.** Add noodles and vegetables you might like to soup pot and cook until all are tender.

Variations

1. Substitute potatoes or rice for noodles. **2.** Consider adding an 8 oz. container of sour cream. Allow the soup to cool to serving temperature and then stir in. **3.** Make dumplings from biscuit dough cut in rounds. When the soup is within half an hour of being done, float dough on top and cover soup pot.

Clam or Fish Chowder, New England

"The Maine State Legislature once passed a resolution outlawing Manhattan clam chowder, and I believe it is still in effect. Nothing against Manhattan, but Mainers think chowder must be white, not red. This is a fine basic recipe, not only for clams but for fish, too, although fish may require a bit more cooking." Lael

Ingredients

4 cups shucked raw clams with juice or 1½ lbs. fish fillets
2 thin slices of salt pork diced in ¼" pieces
1 small onion, diced small
4 cups diced potatoes
1 cup water or just enough to show through potatoes
7 cups milk (half milk and half cream for thicker chowder)

Additions: 3 T. butter with pepper to taste. If you decide to salt, wait until chowder is cooked, because you might discover it is salty enough.

Directions

1. Fry salt pork until brown over low heat in kettle used for chowder. Remove pork and cook onion slowly in pork fat until translucent. **2.** Add potatoes and just enough water to show through at the top. Cover pot, bring to steaming point and lower heat, cooking until potatoes are soft (about 15 minutes). **3.** Stir in cut clams with juice, or fish fillets that are cut into inch-sized pieces. **4.** Season and serve topped with salt pork cubes or saltine crackers.

For Clams: Add to stew and cook for no longer than 3 minutes or they will be tough.

Then add milk and reheat, stirring constantly.

For Fish: Add to chowder and cook over low heat for about 30 minutes. Then add milk and reheat, stirring constantly.

Corn Chowder

"This chowder was traditionally almost as big on New England menus as baked beans, especially during the lush summers when the rustle of corn tassels could actually be heard in our vegetable garden. With biscuits or rolls, the dish can be considered a meal in itself, and it remains a popular favorite." Lael

Ingredients

3–4 pieces of bacon
1 large onion, chopped
2 cups cooked fresh or frozen corn or canned cream style
1 cup diced raw potato
1 cup chicken broth
3 cups milk or light cream

Additions: If you like your chowder thickened, stir 1–2 T. flour during Step two. Some people like little squares of fried salt pork instead of bacon. Either is delicious.

Directions

1. In the bottom of a large kettle, fry bacon or salt pork until crisp. Remove and drain. Remove about half the fat. 2. Sauté onions and potato slowly in remaining fat until onion is yellow. Then add chicken broth and corn. 3. Cover and simmer until corn and potato are tender. Add milk and heat slowly. Stir in crumbled bacon and serve.

Cream of Crab Soup

"Since Linda grew up in Maryland, which is the East Coast heartland of crab cooking, I left her the honor of adding this classic recipe. I was amused to discover, however, it's much the same recipe I use for my native Maine lobster. Except no Old Bay seasoning for tradition-bound 'Maine-acs.' We're purists to the core." Lael

"The first time I went to visit Lael in Maine, actually to work on this book, I fell in love with Saco, where she lived. Her darling home sat right across from the Saco River, sparkling and sapphire in color, and just blocks from the beach with the huge waves I love so much about New England.

"On our way home from the airport, we just casually stopped at a little store and bought a few lobsters to take home and steam for dinner that night. Here in Texas, lobster has to be flown in, if it is to be any good, and it is so expensive it is an occasional treat. There in Maine, buying lobster for dinner was as common as stopping at a fast food drive-through. I love lobster so much, I considered moving there, as there is little as scrumptious as great lobster dipped in melted butter and the lobster bisque you can make the next day." Linda

Ingredients

½ stick butter
1 medium onion, chopped
⅓ cup flour
4 cups light cream
1 lb. lump crabmeat
½ tsp. Old Bay seasoning

Additions: ½ tsp. parsley flakes, 3 T. sherry

Directions

1. Melt butter in pan and add onions. Cook until translucent. **2.** Add flour, seasoning and parsley flakes. Whisk until well blended. **3.** While whisking constantly, add light cream. **4.** Bring just to a boil. **5.** Stir in crabmeat. **6.** Reduce heat to low and cook for 20 minutes, stirring occasionally. **7.** Stir in sherry, if desired. Heat 1-to-2 minutes. **8.** Sprinkle with additional seasoning and serve.

French Onion Soup

"This is a great, inexpensive meal for which it is easy to keep ingredients in hand. If dressed up with a fresh salad and bottle of wine, guests—especially those on diets—may well consider it an elegant offering." Lael

Ingredients

¾ cup onions cut in long, thin pieces
2½ T. flour
1 or more slices of dry bread cut in small squares or use commercial croutons

½ cup cheese grated or more (Gruyere is traditional but cheddar and Monterey Jack will also be fine)
3¾ cups water or beef broth
1½ T. butter

Additions: ½ tsp. Worcestershire sauce.

Directions

1. Sauté onions in butter until golden. Stir in flour. Add water and Worcestershire sauce, if desired. Bring to a boil, stirring occasionally. Cook over high heat for 10 minutes or simmer for an hour. **2.** Place small squares of bread in the serving dish (either individual oven-proof soup dishes or a large oven-proof serving bowl) and sprinkle with half of the grated cheese. **3.** Pour hot soup over cheese and bread. Sprinkle with remaining cheese, brown under broiler. **4.** Remove from oven and let stand 6 minutes before serving.

Lemon Egg Soup

"Growing up, we Armenians called this offering 'sick soup,' because any time someone became ill, a pot of this delicious antidote simmered on the stove all day, and it worked to cure all kinds of ills. It is so scrumptious a concoction, though, that you will want it more often. You will find yourself secretly wishing for someone to take to their bed." Linda

Ingredients

4 cups chicken broth
1 cup egg noodles, very fine
2 eggs
1 tsp. salt
1 tsp. pepper 1 lemon, juiced or ¼ cup lemon juice (more if you want it tangier)

Directions

1. Cook noodles in broth until soft. **2.** Beat the eggs; add the lemon juice and beat again. **3.** Add some of the hot broth to the egg/lemon mixture, and beat again. Repeat. **4.** Pour the egg/lemon mixture very slowly into the large pot of soup, mixing all the while so the egg won't curdle. **5.** Reheat the soup on low.

Lentil Soup

"I remember so clearly how the church of my childhood observed Lent, the 40 days beginning Ash Wednesday and ending Holy Thursday. It was considered a time for penance and fasting before celebrating Easter. As a family, we gave up eating meat, so beans and legumes became an important part of our diet, particularly lentils. You would think I might have been turned off, but I love them still in all forms—soups, stews, and salads." Linda

Ingredients

1 onion, diced
3 T. oil
1 cup lentils
5½ cups water
⅓ cup rice
1 cup tomato sauce

Directions

1. In a soup pot, sauté onion in oil. **2.** Add washed lentils and water, and cook until almost tender (about ½ hour). Do not drain. **3.** Add the rice and tomato sauce. **4.** Season with salt and pepper.

Pea Soup

"This inexpensive staple of the financially challenged is so delicious that you'll want to keep it in your menu, even if you hit the jackpot. It tastes even better as a leftover and freezes beautifully in serving-sized portions." Linda

"I like ham, but the main reason I lie in wait for it to go on sale is so I can have an inexpensive ham bone for this recipe. I was raised with a large number of French Canadian neighbors who had wonderful variations of this dish. Oh, to return and again be invited to dine on one of their specialties. But I still love the basic version, too. What beautiful simplicity!" Lael

Ingredients

1 cup dried split green peas
5 cups boiling water
1 onion, chopped fairly fine
2 carrots, peeled and sliced in rounds
2 potatoes, peeled and chopped
1 ham bone (hopefully with some ham still left on it, or just throw in chunks of ham)

Additions: 1 T. garlic salt, 1 tsp. pepper, just a pinch of powdered cloves, and some cooks like to float bread croutons on each serving.

Directions

1. Pick over peas for discolored ones and small stones and then rinse thoroughly to remove all dirt. **2.** Combine 3 cups of boiling water with remaining ingredients in a pot. Cook covered on medium heat for 20 minutes, stirring after 10 minutes. **3.** Cover and cook for 25 minutes, adding remaining water as needed. Or cook at a slower speed in crockpot until peas are mashable and meat is tender. **4.** Remove soup bone, cut off any meat that has not fallen off, return meat to soup, and discard the bone. **5.** Mix thoroughly before serving.

Potato Soup

"This is an elegant version of a poor man's necessity from my past." Lael

Ingredients
5 potatoes, peeled and cubed
5 cubes chicken bouillon
2 quarts water
1 pinch ground nutmeg
1 pint heavy whipping cream
3 green onions, chopped

Additions: salt and pepper to taste, 1 tsp. garlic salt, bacon bits, ham bits, shredded cheddar cheese to top.

Directions
1. In a large pot over high heat, combine the potatoes, bouillon, water, salt and pepper, garlic salt and nutmeg. Cook for about 15 minutes or until potatoes are tender. **2.** Add the heavy cream and the green onions. Stir well and allow soup to bubble up, about 5 minutes.

Pumpkin Soup

"I discovered this recipe when I was living in the West Indies where pumpkin is a staple, and I found how grand this inexpensive basic can be." Lael

Ingredients
3 T. butter
½ cup chopped onions
2 cups pumpkin puree
   (fresh or canned)
3 cups chicken broth
½ cup light cream
¼ tsp. sugar

Additions: 1 tsp. salt, dash of pepper, dash of nutmeg, and maybe a dollop of sour cream.

Directions
1. Heat butter in pot. Add onion and gently sauté for 10 minutes. **2.** Add pumpkin puree, salt, nutmeg, and pepper. **3.** Slowly stir in chicken broth. Heat through, then gradually stir in cream.

Tomato Basil Soup

"For the first seven years of my life, I actually believed that Campbell's Tomato Soup was the only soup in the world. I still love it but how excited I was to learn there were other ways to go." Lael

Ingredients

1 cup heavy cream or light cream
¼ lb. sweet butter
4 cups tomatoes, peeled, cored, chopped or 4 cups canned whole tomatoes, crushed
4 cups chicken stock (or broth)
12 fresh basil leaves (washed and snipped into small pieces) or ½ tsp. dried basil or ½ tsp. mixed Italian herbs

Directions

1. Combine stock and tomatoes in pot. Simmer approximately 40 minutes for fresh tomatoes, 15 minutes for canned. **2.** Puree in blender or processor. Add basil leaves in small amounts to liquid being processed. **3.** Return to saucepan and add cream and butter; stir over low heat.

U.S. Senate Bean Soup

"Republican Senator Henry Cabot Lodge, Sr. from Massachusetts, is credited with introducing this recipe but, according to legend, it was Senators Fred Thomas Dubois of Idaho and Knute Nelson of Minnesota who authored a resolution giving it a permanent place on the U.S. Senate dining room menu." Lael

Ingredients

1 cup dried peas or navy beans
10 cups water
1 ham bone with meat
2 medium onions, finely chopped
2 cups celery, chopped
1¼ cups mashed potatoes

Additions: 1 garlic clove, minced, 1 T. chopped parsley, and 2 T. butter.

Directions

1. Soak beans in 4 cups water overnight, and then drain. (For faster preparation, add beans to boiling water and continue to boil over high heat for 2 minutes. Remove beans from heat, cover and let stand 1 hour before draining). **2.** About 3 hours before serving, boil beans and bone in 6 cups of water. Reduce heat to low, cover and simmer 1½ hours or until beans are tender. **3.** Add remaining ingredients and simmer uncovered over low heat for 30 minutes. **4.** Remove bone, cut meat from it and discard. Return meat in bite-sized pieces to stew. Simmer, uncovered until soup thickens to the desired consistency.

Vegetable Soup

"This is a good, basic recipe to which you can add any veggie of a similar nature plus luxuries like meat and seafood." Lael

Ingredients

1 medium onion, diced (about 1 cup)
1 large carrot, peeled and diced (about 1 cup)
½ cup dried apricots, diced
1 cup lentils or black beans or cannellini beans
4 cups vegetable or chicken broth

Directions

1. Sauté onions over high heat about 1 minute or until they begin to soften. Put into a stew or crockpot with carrots, lentils, and broth and bring to a boil. **2.** Add apricot pieces and simmer until lentils are tender (about 25 minutes). Do not overcook. **3.** Serve hot.

Variations

Add 1 cup chopped chicken and other vegetables like zucchini, potatoes and/or corn.

Tips for Scrumptious Soups, Stews, and Chowders

1. Adding salt early when you cook stews and soups is better because it flavors the entire pot rather than just the top layer as when salting at the table. If you add too much salt to a pot, add a spoonful of sugar or put in a raw potato to absorb the excess, then discard the potato.

2. If you've made anything too sweet, add salt or cider vinegar. Use fresh instead of processed spices and herbs when possible because they contain higher levels of antioxidants and curative properties. Buy spices whole and grind them before use; crush dried leaves or herbs, and use whole sprigs in long-cooking dishes for maximum benefit.

3. To eliminate fat from stews, soups, or gravies, refrigerate overnight. The fat will rise to the top and harden. Skim off all that is white or yellow. If you don't have time to refrigerate, lay pieces of bread on top of the pot one at a time and let them absorb oil.

4. Bone broth is healthier for you and much richer in flavor. Boil all beef, chicken, and turkey bones on low until they are leached of color. You can add onions, herbs like bay leaf and rosemary, and other vegetables, including celery and carrots, as you make stock for even more flavor. The stock can be used for beef, chicken, or turkey soup or it can be the base of other soups and casseroles.

5. Get creative with your soup stock. Add a cup of rice (brown or black) for a healthy carbohydrate. Add beans (pinto, black, navy, cannellini, red, or ranch style beans) to your soup stock for a healthy and lower calorie protein, or noodles for texture and flavor.

6. Soup stock freezes well, so if you make too much, freeze for another meal. You can also freeze stock in ice cube trays, so you can pop them out later to enhance the flavors of sauces and gravies.

7. If your soup or stew needs to be thickened, there are a variety of tricks using pureeing as the method: Puree a few cups of your sauce or stew, then add it back in, and it will naturally thicken your dish. Depending of the kind of soup or stew, add pureed sweet potato, pumpkin, acorn or butternut squash for a delicious thickener. Pureed potatoes, carrots, and parsnips also work well.

8. Add the rinds of cheeses, especially Parmesan, to your soup, sauce, or stew for extra flavoring. Remove before serving.

9. Add V-8 juice instead of tomato sauce for tangier flavor.

ENTREES

"*Dinner on the table at six o'clock with everyone in the family present was a tradition in our home. It was when we shared our day with each other, discussed issues, explored and solved problems, and expressed gratitude for the bounty before us. It was also the opportunity to tame the wild beast—teaching kids good manners, the social graces, and the art of adult conversation.*

"Dinner with its substantive entrée, healthy salad, vegetable side, and sweet dessert was the perfect ending to the day and a great precursor to the evening ahead. The entrée was always the star, though. It anchored the rest of the meal that included complementary side dishes. Get the entrée perfect and the rest is smooth sailing.

"Dinner was most certainly the celebration of the family that was served up with love and healthy, delicious food." Linda

Beef Brisket

"Texans take their barbecue very seriously. It had better be cooked long and on low, and be tender enough to be "pulled." Pulled pork was a new term to me when I moved to Texas thirty years ago, but I sure loved the barbecue sandwiches that were piled high with brisket so tender, shredding it was done easily with a fork." Linda

Ingredients
4 lb. beef brisket
2 T. seasoned salt
2 T. black pepper
2 T. garlic salt

8 T. Worcestershire sauce
1 bottle of good, dark barbecue sauce

Directions
1. Rub seasoning over beef. Place beef, fat side up, in 13 x 9" foil pan. Cover with foil and refrigerate overnight. **2.** Cook in a 200° oven for 8–10 hours. **3.** Before the last hour, pour bottle of barbecue sauce over beef. Re-cover and continue cooking. **4.** Remove from pan and let stand for 10 minutes before cutting. That process ensures that juices remain in the meat. Slice on an angle and serve with pan sauce.

Beef Stroganoff

"Beef Stroganoff is a Russian dish of sautéed pieces of beef served in a sauce with Smetana, the name for various sour creams from Central and Eastern Europe. Smetana is a dairy product produced by souring heavy cream. Similar to crème fraîche (28% fat), today it is sold with 10% to 30% milkfat content, depending on the country. Beef Stroganoff, with its origins in mid-nineteenth-century, has become popular around the world, though with considerable variation from the original recipe. This is an elegant classic that can be served either with cooked noodles or rice." Linda

Ingredients

1 lb. round steak, ¼" to ½" thick
3 oz. can or ⅔ cup sliced mushrooms
1 pkg. onion soup mix
1 cup sour cream
⅔ cup water
2 T. flour

Directions

1. Trim fat from meat and save it. Cut meat diagonally across the grain in ¼" strips. **2.** Heat fat in skillet and brown meat strips. Add water and sliced mushrooms, including liquid if you are using canned variety. **3.** Stir in onion soup mix and heat just to boiling. Blend sour cream with flour and add to beef mixture. Cook until it thickens, stirring all the while. Sauce will be thin. **4.** Serve hot over cooked rice or noodles.

Brunch Casserole

"This recipe makes a great standby for emergencies. Most of the ingredients are items I always keep on hand." Lael

Ingredients

1, 8 oz. can of crescent rolls
2 cups shredded
  mozzarella cheese
4 eggs, beaten

1 lb. spicy bulk sausage
¾ cup milk
Dash of basil

Additions: 1 tsp. salt, ½ tsp. pepper

Directions

1. Cook sausage and drain. **2.** Line bottom of greased 13 x 9 x 2" glass dish that is oven proof with rolls, pressing perforations to seal. **3.** Sprinkle with sausage and cheese. **4.** Combine remaining ingredients; beat well and pour over sausage. **5.** Bake at 425° for 15 minutes or until set. Let stand 5 minutes; cut and serve.

Chicken Parmesan

"My family loves this dish. I wanted to make crispy, flavorful chicken without the extra calories and fat in the skin, so this is what I created. The cheese crisps up enough that you don't even notice the chicken is sans skin." Linda

Ingredients

2 lbs. chicken (breasts or
  thighs), skin removed
2 eggs, beaten

½ cup Parmesan cheese
¼ tsp. ground red pepper
½ tsp. garlic salt

Directions

1. Mix cheese with spices. **2.** Dip chicken in egg. **3.** Coat with cheese mixture. **4.** Broil until brown on one side and turn over. Broil until brown.

Chicken Cacciatore

"I have been lucky to travel the world. I have visited more than thirty-five countries and found, in each one, delicacies that were to die for. My writing partner, Lael, says I ate myself around the world, and that is really the truth.

"You won't be surprised by this, but I found the best food in Italy. Perhaps it was the ambience of butterflies and water wheels in Assisi or the drama of gondolas and gypsies in Venice, or the miracle of Michelangelo at every turn in Florence that made everything we ate taste better, but the pizza was aromatic bread that oozed with cheese, and the pasta swam in sauces that we wanted to lick from the plate, and the gelato was the coldest, sweetest ice cream we'd ever tasted.

"Chicken Cacciatore is a classic Italian dish, a succulent hunter stew in which chicken or rabbit is braised in a sauce with mushrooms, onions, garlic, white wine, and spices including thyme, parsley, and oregano. The original version, which was once cooked outdoors over an open fire, resulted in brown gravy. Today, it is cooked indoors with raised instead of game chicken and in a thick, well spiced, red sauce that is perfect over spaghetti or angel hair pasta." *Linda*

Ingredients

⅓ cup olive oil
3 lb. frying chicken, cut up
1 medium onion, thinly sliced
1 large green pepper, cut into ¼" strips
1 tsp. oregano
Spaghetti sauce (recipe in Index).
Addition: ½ cup white wine to the spaghetti sauce.

Directions

1. Heat oil in large skillet and fry chicken on all sides until golden brown. **2.** Push chicken to one side. Add onions and green pepper and sauté. **3.** Redistribute chicken, onions and green pepper, and cover in thick, well-spiced spaghetti sauce. **4.** Add extra oregano. **5.** Simmer covered for 30–40 minutes or until chicken is tender.

Chicken Dinner, in Foil or Tin Can

"Before the invention of plastic lids, we used to plop the ingredients for a "hobo dinner" into a washed coffee can, top with its tin lid, and toss it into the oven or a campfire for an hour or so for an easy and inexpensive meal.

"Today you can purchase heavy foil bags which work in conventional ovens but may not survive camp fires unless wrapped twice in heavy tin foil and buried in glowing coals. Some of us still use a large tin can with a tin lid if we can find one to fit. In any case, foil dinners are delicious and easy, especially in terms of clean-up." Lael

Ingredients

5 small potatoes, peeled and sliced
4 chicken breasts
6 link sausages
1 tsp. poultry seasoning
1 onion, chopped
1 can peas or bag of frozen peas

Additions: Cherry tomatoes, corn, green pepper, mushrooms and/or carrots, plus seasonings and maybe a dash of wine.

Directions

1. Preheat oven to 400°, or build camp fire and let it burn down to hot coals. **2.** Slice potatoes thick. **3.** Place all ingredients, chicken first, in a meal-sized metal can with tight metal cover or commercial heavy foil bag. Seal foil bag or cover can. If using a conventional oven, place on a cookie sheet and bake for an hour. For campfire, bury in coals and check in about an hour.

Variation

This is also delicious with sausage and potatoes, carrots and onions.

Chicken for Dummies

"The story surrounding the name was simple. When the cook asked what the family wanted for Sunday dinner, her reply to them was—"not that dumb chicken dish again." This ridiculously easy recipe will yield six portions of succulent chicken, vegetables, and delicious gravy. If you're going to entertain a dozen or more people, just double the recipe—beginning with two frozen chickens." Linda

Ingredients

1 whole chicken, frozen or thawed
6 potatoes, scrubbed, unpeeled, and cut in quarters
½ lb. carrots, scrubbed, unpeeled, and cut in 2" sections

1 onion, cut in rings
2, 10.5 oz. cans condensed cream of chicken soup, plus ½ can of water
2, 10.5 oz. cans condensed cream of mushroom soup, plus ½ can of water

Additions: 1 tsp. pepper, 1 T. garlic salt

Directions

1. Preheat oven to 400° or use crockpot. 2. Put one whole chicken in a roasting pan or crockpot with a lid. Do not remove the giblets. Just leave them in to flavor things. 3. Add potatoes to the pan with carrots. 4. Lay onion rings around the top of everything. 5. Season all that is in the pan with pepper, onion, and garlic salt. Then add soups. Just slop on top with water. 6. Cover the roasting pan tightly and bake or simmer for 3 to 4 hours.

Variation

Use chicken parts instead of a whole chicken, add cream to sauce to thicken even further, and instead of using potatoes, serve with rice pilaf.

Chicken Fried Steak

"This dish is a favorite in Southwestern and Plains states, not only because of its delightful flavor, but because it is a good way to stretch steak (quite literally, since the meat is pounded thin to cook quickly). This recipe also produces gravy which goes well with mashed potatoes or biscuits. I'd never tried it until I moved to Texas, but it became my favorite recipe from that great republic." Lael

Ingredients

1 ½ lbs. beef top round steak cut ½" thick
¾ cup flour
¼ cup vegetable oil
2 cups milk or light cream
Salt and pepper to taste

Directions

1. Trim fat from steak and cut into six servings, removing any bone. **2.** Mix ½ cup flour and seasonings in bowl and then on a cutting board, pound flour mixture into both sides of steak with meat mallet until flour is absorbed and meat is about ⅛" thick. (If you don't have a meat mallet, try using a rolling pin end down, after unscrewing one of the handles.) **3.** Heat oil in frying pan over medium heat and cook steaks until well browned on both sides, turning once. **4.** Remove steaks and keep them warm while you stir the remaining flour into oil until smooth. Then gradually stir in milk and cook stirring constantly until mixture boils. **5.** Top steaks with gravy. There should be enough also to pour over potatoes or biscuits.

Chicken Salad

"A versatile dish, chopped chicken works with whatever is in the refrigerator—cooked vegetables including chopped broccoli, cauliflower, and/or carrots. Add shredded or cubed cheese, chopped pimento or pickle, or black or green olives. Replace chicken with chopped turkey or roast (though when you do this with roast, try a creamy Italian or Ranch dressing). With all other combinations, you can use the oil and vinegar dressing." Linda

Ingredients

Leftover chicken, chopped in cubes or shredded
Cherry or grape tomatoes, halved
Green onions, chopped
Craisins
Salad greens, (romaine, red leaf or iceberg lettuce), chopped into pieces
Garlic salt and pepper

Directions

1. Combine ingredients. **2.** Pour on favorite dressing and mix salad. Serve immediately.

Variation

Add diced onion, celery, and garlic to 2 cups chopped or shredded chicken. Combine ½ cup mayonnaise with salt, pepper, and a tsp. of vinegar and add to chicken. Mix thoroughly and refrigerate before serving.

Chicken Spaghetti

"Because I grew up on the East Coast, I thought the only color spaghetti could be was red. It was certainly the only kind my mother made. It was after I moved to Texas that I learned that spaghetti could be golden in color, too, and so very delicious. After going to several events that served the dish with Texas pride, I asked the best Southern cook I knew for the recipe. It is a great dish to take to large gatherings because it can feed a horde—even a small serving is filling, and it freezes beautifully." Linda

Ingredients

4 oz. spaghetti, broken into 2" pieces
2, 10.5 oz. cans condensed cream of mushroom soup, undiluted
1 cup milk

2 cups cooked, chopped chicken
1/3 cup onions, chopped
8 oz. sharp cheddar cheese, shredded

Addition: add 3 oz. can sliced mushrooms, with liquid.

Directions

1. Preheat oven to 350°. **2.** Cook and drain spaghetti. **3.** Mix soup and milk. **4.** Add onions, mushrooms, chicken and mix. **5.** Add cheese but reserve 1/2 cup for topping. **6.** Pour into 1 1/2 quart greased casserole and top with the cheese. **7.** Bake for 45 minutes.

Chili

"A dish made all over the country, this winter staple is cause for controversy. Those in the Southwest are pretty adamant that "real" chili is made without beans. They're so partial to their meat-based concoction that they've honored it with cowboy stories and songs.

Back East, beans are an important ingredient, and they still grace my recipe, but I've lived in Texas for the last thirty years, and so I've come to appreciate chili without as well. However, my recipe has also resulted in many cowboy converts!" Linda

Ingredients
1 lb. ground chuck beef
1 T. olive oil
1 onion, diced
32 oz. can of diced tomatoes
3, 16 oz. cans of red kidney beans
2 T. chili powder (or more for greater kick)

Additions: 2 cloves chopped garlic, salt, pepper and serve with grated cheese, diced onions and saltine crackers

Directions
1. Sauté onions and garlic in oil in large pot. **2.** Add beef and brown, breaking up the meat through the process of browning. **3.** Add tomatoes. **4.** Add kidney beans and spices. **5.** Cook for 4 hours. Stir often and skim any fat before serving.

Corned Beef and Cabbage

"When the Irish immigrated to America, they brought a number of delicious dishes with them, including soda bread and Irish stew. The Irish preferred cooking with pork, particularly Irish bacon, but, believe it or not, pork in America then was far more expensive than beef, the staple in the American diet.

"Many of the Irish working class in New York frequented Jewish delicatessens where they were first introduced to corned beef. Because it cooked much like Irish bacon and was tasty, they began using it as they had the bacon. Cabbage was also more inexpensive than potatoes, a staple in the old country, and was the perfect balance to the spiced and salty beef. And they could be cooked at the same time in the same pot. The ease and heartiness were as perfect a match as the meat and vegetable." Linda

Ingredients

1 corned beef (a vacuum-sealed beef that is about 4.5 lbs. works well)
1 medium head of cabbage
⅔ cup honey
½ cup pickling spice mix (McCormick and Durkee both have good spice combinations), wrapped and tied in cheese cloth or in a large tea ball

Directions

1. Put corned beef in a 6–8 quart, heavy bottomed, stock pot filled with cold water, ¾ full. Bring to a boil and cook for 5 minutes. **2.** Remove beef and rinse off foam with cool water. **3.** Wash stock pot thoroughly and fill again with cold water, ¾ full. **4.** Put beef in pot with honey and pickling spice mix. **5.** Roast must float in the pot at all times. Turn roast over every hour so that all sides cook evenly. Cook over medium heat for several hours until tender. **6.** When tender, remove roast and place in an ovenproof dish to keep warm while cooking cabbage. **7.** Remove and discard spices from pot. Then add enough water to cook cabbage. **8.** Quarter cabbage into wedges and place into the pot. Cook until tender.

Croquettes

"My mother warned me never to eat croquettes in a restaurant because they might be made of leftovers, and heaven only knew how old. However, I love this dish and when I make it myself, I don't have to worry. Consider serving it with gravy." Lael

Ingredients

2 T. butter, plus additional for greasing baking tin
2 T. flour, plus 1 cup in which to roll croquettes
1 cup milk
2 cups ground or chopped cooked meat
2 eggs, slightly beaten, added one at a time
1½ cup dry breadcrumbs

Additions: ¼ tsp. grated onion, ¼ cup chopped mushrooms, 1 tsp. Worcestershire sauce, 2 T. chopped parsley, and/or ½ tsp. nutmeg.

Directions

1. Melt 2 T. butter in pan and stir in flour. Slowly stir in milk and keep stirring until mixture thickens. Stir in 1 beaten egg. **2.** Add meat and other extras, if desired. **3.** Remove from heat and chill thoroughly. **4.** Preheat oven to 350°. **5.** Divide mixture into 12 sections and shape into balls or like sugarplums. Dip in flour, then in beaten egg, and finally dry breadcrumbs. **6.** Place on greased baking tin and cook for 45 minutes. **7.** Serve hot.

Variation

You can deep fry the croquettes if you don't like the untraditional baking method.

Dolma or Stuffed Cabbage

"I grew up eating stuffed vegetables or "Dolma". It was and is still an intricate part of the Mediterranean diet. The dish is full of vitamins and minerals and very low in fat and calories, especially if you drain the browned meat before adding the other ingredients.

Tomatoes, bell peppers, squash, and zucchini all lend themselves beautifully to this dish. My dad's favorite was stuffed green peppers and mine was stuffed cabbage, but unlike the other vegetables, that dish took a lot more time and work, and the pungent aroma of cooking cabbage filled the house. I loved the dish so much, though, that I had to come up with a short cut. Honestly, the Variation below tastes as good, if not better, because it is easy and takes almost no time to make." Linda

Ingredients

1 onion, chopped
1 cup converted or brown rice
3 lbs. ground chuck
1 head of cabbage
1, 48 oz. can of chicken broth
1, 32 oz. can of chopped tomatoes

Additions: 2 tsp. salt, 1 tsp. black pepper, 1 T. chopped garlic. Plain yogurt is a delicious topping.

Directions

1. Mix thoroughly the onion, spices, and rice into the raw meat. **2.** Boil the cabbage leaves just until limp. Then drain. **3.** Stuff each leaf with a portion of the meat mixture and roll up tightly. **4.** Stack cabbage rolls in pot and add chicken broth and tomatoes. **5.** Cook on low heat for 1 hour.

Variation: Stuffed Cabbage without the Stuffing

1. Sauté 1 chopped onion and 1 T. chopped garlic in 1 T. olive oil. **2.** Add meat and brown thoroughly while breaking it into small pieces. **3.** Add 1 cup rice and a small bag of shredded cabbage (normally used for coleslaw). **4.** Add 1, 32 oz. can of chopped tomatoes and 1, 48 oz. can of chicken broth. **5.** Simmer until cabbage is cooked.

Fish Baked in Sour Cream

"This is my favorite of all Linda's recipes. I tried it first with a lemon that was well past its prime and, yet, the dish was marvelous. It also works with fish that is not expensive. It is the same as money in the bank." Lael

Ingredients
1½ lb. fish fillets
1 lemon cut in thin slices
5 sprigs parsley

1 cup sour cream
¼ tsp. onion salt
Worcestershire sauce

Additions: paprika or nutmeg

Directions
1. Preheat oven to 400°. **2.** Put parsley and lemon slices in bottom of a greased baking dish, and top with fish. **3.** Cover dish and bake 25 minutes. **4.** Mix sour cream with onion salt and a drop or two of Worcestershire sauce. Spread over fish, top with paprika, if desired, and broil until lightly brown and bubbly.

Variations
1. Dip fish in egg wash. **2.** Dredge in instant mashed potatoes (for a real fish and chips flavor) or dip in Parmesan cheese or diced nuts. **3.** Sauté on each side until brown.

Fish Poached in Lemon Milk

"This recipe has the advantage of a short cooking time and results in a delightfully moist entrée." Lael

Ingredients
1 lb. fish (cod or haddock fillets)
2 ½ cups water
2 T. nonfat dry milk
2 T. lemon juice
½ lemon, peeled and sliced

Directions
1. Cut fillets into serving-size portions. **2.** Mix water, dry milk, and lemon juice. Bring liquid to a boil. Reduce heat to just under boiling. **3.** Slide fillets into liquid. Simmer about 5 minutes. (Cook 10 minutes for every inch of thickness at the thickest part of the fish.) **4.** Remove from liquid carefully to avoid breaking pieces. **5.** Garnish with lemon slices.

Fried Chicken

"Recipes for this favorite vary throughout the South, but traditionalists agree on two points. The bird should be marinated in buttermilk eight to ten hours before frying, and pieces should be coated in a spiced flour mixture that contains no corn meal." Lael

Ingredients

8 pieces of chicken (consider drumsticks and thighs)
3 cups buttermilk
1 ½ cups flour
2 tsp. salt
½ tsp. cayenne pepper
Vegetable oil

Directions

1. Coat chicken pieces with buttermilk, cover and marinate in the refrigerator at least 8 hours. **2.** Combine dry ingredients in plastic bag. **3.** Drain chicken, wiping off most of the buttermilk. Pop pieces in bag with flour mixture, a few pieces at a time. Coat pieces well with flour, remove from bag and place on a rack to dry. **4.** Heat 1" of oil in a heavy frying pan to about 350°. Fry chicken over medium heat about 20 to 25 minutes until crisp and golden brown. Drain pieces on paper towels before serving.

Fried Chicken in the Oven

"When you're craving 'Southern Fried' chicken, this is another way to go. It is less greasy than the traditional version, but still an energy provider in cold weather." Lael

Ingredients
1 small chicken cut in pieces
3 cups breadcrumbs
1 ½ cups vegetable oil
Seasoning of your choice (oregano, seasoned salt, pepper)

Directions
1. Heat oven to 350°. **2.** Put breadcrumbs and spices in bag big enough to shake chicken pieces in. **3.** Put oil in shallow dish and dip chicken pieces in it. **4.** Drain oiled chicken pieces, place in breadcrumb bag and shake until well coated. **5.** Place chicken pieces in baking dish and bake for 1 hour.

Ham Hocks and Black-Eyed Peas

"A friend from the South, who is a mother of five, shared this amazing recipe, warning me never to cook it for anyone I didn't love, as I'd never get rid of the person. She was right. It's also a perfect recipe for a crockpot." Lael

Ingredients

1 cup black-eyed peas
1 lb. ham hocks
2 onions, chopped
1 clove garlic, minced
1 small can tomato puree
Boiling water

Additions: 2 celery stalks, diced; one hot red pepper, diced; one small bay leaf; and 2 T. chili sauce.

Directions

1. Put peas in water to cover and boil for 2 minutes. Turn off heat and let stand for an hour. **2.** In a separate pan, put ham hocks in water enough to cover and boil for 30 minutes. **3.** Drain peas and combine with meat and cooking water. Add the rest of the ingredients and simmer until tender (2–4 hours).

Italian Meatballs

"*Packaged meatballs are good and inexpensive, especially if you buy them at the big box stores. So good, in fact, it is easy to forget that they are better yet and even cheaper if you make them from scratch.*" Lael

"*Though I have suggested making my meatballs with spaghetti, remember they are delicious on crusty bread for meatball sandwiches, and, if you stick in a toothpick, you have a delicious appetizer. They also freeze well.*" Linda

Ingredients

3 garlic cloves, minced or
   1 T. garlic salt
1 onion, chopped fine and
   sautéed with garlic in
   1 T. olive oil

1 lb. ground chuck
¾ cup Italian breadcrumbs
1 egg
Spaghetti sauce
   (recipe in the Index)

Additions: ½ cup Parmesan cheese or finely grated Romano cheese, ½ can of V-8, salt and pepper to taste.

Directions

1. Mix all ingredients for meatballs, shape into balls and brown in vegetable oil. **2.** Add browned meatballs to spaghetti sauce, and cook in nonstick frying pan over medium heat for ½ hour or bake in an oven at 350° for the same amount of time.

Kapusta (ribs and sauerkraut)

"I've always liked sauerkraut so much that it is hard for me to understand that it is also good for you. The name of this Polish dish, which so handsomely incorporates it, translates to "cabbage," and I view the recipe as a national treasure." Lael

Ingredients
1, 32 oz. jar of sauerkraut
1 large onion, chopped
1 whole garlic, chopped
2, 14 oz. cans of chicken broth
2 lbs. country pork ribs
½ lb. bacon, cubed and cooked

Directions
1. Preheat oven to 250–300°. **2.** Drain and squeeze sauerkraut until all juice is gone. **3.** Place pork in bottom of baking pan and cover with dry sauerkraut, onions, and garlic. **4.** Cover and bake for 2 hours. **5.** Uncover and bake 2–3 hours more, turning caramelized sauerkraut and onions into the pork. Pork should start breaking down and blending in with mixture. About every hour into this, add chicken broth and stir and keep baking. **6.** Add cooked, cubed bacon for the last 1½ hours of baking, adding some bacon grease as well to hold things together. Add chicken broth as often and as much as you like to obtain desired juiciness.

Lamb Chops

"When I moved to Texas, I was shocked at how difficult it was to buy lamb chops—30 years ago, almost impossible. Texans like their beef and think they don't like lamb. In fact, many, at that time, had never tasted a lamb chop, including a good friend of mine who was otherwise an excellent cook. I invited her over for sautéed chicken livers (something else she'd never tasted) and broiled lamb chops. She was an immediate convert. The recipe below is excellent served with pilaf." Linda

Ingredients

2 lbs. lamb chops
1 T. olive oil
1 medium onion, sliced
1 tomato, diced
2 cloves garlic, minced
¼ tsp. dried thyme leaves

Directions

1. Heat olive oil in skillet. Add lamb, onion, tomato, garlic, and thyme. **2.** Cover and cook over very low heat at least 1½ hours.

Variations

1. Instead of the above, sprinkle lamb chops with seasoning salt and broil until brown on each side. Then serve with mint jelly.
2. Or bake lamb chops and eggplant for about an hour. First remove eggplant stem and cut into ¼" rounds. Soak in salt water for 15 minutes. Pat dry and brush with oil. Arrange in pan, cover with sliced onion, and bake at 350° for ½ hour, then add 1 cup canned tomatoes, chopped. Lay the lamb chops on top and salt and pepper to taste. Turn lamb chops when brown. Salt and pepper the other side and brown.

Lazy Lasagna

"Lasagna from scratch can be a lot of work. I'm not fond of most commercial varieties which are high in sodium and usually taste a bit 'wooden.' So I was delighted when Linda introduced this recipe which is not only quick and easy but as tasty as more complicated recipes that take much longer to assemble." Lael

Ingredients

14 oz. box of ziti or bowtie pasta
16 oz. pkg. mozzarella cheese
16 oz. carton of large curd cottage or ricotta cheese
1 cup Parmesan cheese
3 T. garlic salt
Spaghetti sauce (recipe in Index)

Directions

1. Preheat oven to 330°. **2.** Cook and drain pasta. **3.** Spray a pan with nonstick spray, and lay out the first layer of noodles. **4.** Pour on ⅓ of the spaghetti sauce. **5.** Spoon on ⅓ of the cottage cheese so it covers the layer of noodles. **6.** Slice mozzarella and lay several pieces on the cottage cheese, so that when they melt, they will cover the entire layer. **7.** Sprinkle mozzarella with ⅓ cup Parmesan cheese and 1 T. garlic salt. **8.** Repeat two more layers with the last of the Parmesan on top. **9.** Cook for 1½ hours.

Macaroni and Cheese

"This recipe comes from the Congressional Club cookbook of 1987, complete with a foreword by Nancy Reagan. Her husband, then president, contributed his favorite recipe, found below and elegant in its simplicity. We found macaroni and cheese to be THE favorite with the majority of those surveyed on their most loved comfort foods." Lael

Ingredients

½ lb. macaroni
1 tsp. butter plus additional for greasing pan
1 egg, beaten

2½ cups sharp cheese, grated plus ½ cup for topping dish
1 T. hot water
1 cup milk

Additions: 1 tsp. dry mustard to mix with macaroni and some fine bread crumbs to add to the topping.

Directions

1. Cook macaroni according to directions on pkg. until almost done and drain thoroughly. **2.** Preheat oven to 350°. **3.** Stir butter, egg, and 2½ cups cheese into macaroni and place in buttered casserole dish. **4.** Mix hot water, milk and mustard if desired. Pour over macaroni and top with ½ cup cheese. **5.** Bake 45 minutes or until custard is set and top crusty.

Maryland Crab Cakes

"Making great crab cakes is considered an art form in Maryland. I know because I grew up there. Nothing was more pleasurable than seeking out the restaurants that made the best crab cakes during our sometimes weekly trips to the Chesapeake Bay and Ocean City.

"Often those restaurants were nothing more than dilapidated shacks (inspiration for the name Joe's Crab Shack) hidden in some hamlet along the shore, but the ambiance didn't diminish the succulent lumps of blue crab meat or the sweetness of the soft-shelled crabs, often eaten in their entirety. There are as many crab cake recipes as crabs in the Chesapeake, but I like this one for its simplicity." Linda

Ingredients

1 lb. crabmeat
1 cup Italian seasoned breadcrumbs
1 large egg
¼ cup mayonnaise
1 tsp. dry mustard
Oil for frying

Additions: 1 tsp. Worcestershire sauce, salt and pepper to taste

Directions

1. Remove all cartilage from crabmeat. **2.** Mix breadcrumbs, egg, mayonnaise, and seasonings. **3.** Add crabmeat and mix gently but thoroughly. If mixture is too dry, add a little more mayonnaise. **4.** Shape into 6 cakes and fry in just enough oil to prevent sticking. Cook for about 5 minutes on each side.

Meatloaf

"Through the ages, most civilizations have served various sorts of meat loaves. They became particularly popular in America, beginning with the Great Depression. Cooks were able to stretch cheaper meats by adding fillers like bread crumbs and oats. Meatloaf was a hardy meal that people could serve their families during what was the most difficult economic time in our history.

"It grew in popularity again during World War II. The objective was to get as much nutrition on the table for as little money as possible. When meat rationing began, vegetarian options were created." *Linda*

Ingredients
2 lbs. ground chuck
1 ½ cup soft breadcrumbs
2 eggs
¾ cup water
1 envelope onion soup mix
½ cup ketchup (or substitute with ½ cup V-8 juice for a healthier and tangier version)

Directions
1. Preheat oven to 350°. **2.** Mix all ingredients thoroughly with your clean hands. **3.** Bake in a loaf pan for 1 hour.

Pasta Alfredo

"A good Alfredo sauce is delicious on steamed vegetables and any kind of pasta, though most people pour it over fettuccine (hence the name Fettuccine Alfredo). I love this luscious sauce on angel hair pasta." Linda

Ingredients

¼ lb. butter
2 cups light cream
1 cup Parmesan cheese (add more if you like thick sauce)
1 T. garlic salt
1 tsp. black pepper
½ lb. fettucine or 1 box bowtie noodles or ½ lb. angel hair pasta

Directions

1. Melt butter; add cream, cheese, garlic salt, and pepper. **2.** Mix thoroughly and cook until just thickened. **3.** Pour over pasta and serve immediately.

Variation:
Ingredients

8 oz. noodles or other pasta
1 envelope Italian salad dressing mix
1 T. chopped parsley
½ cup cream or evaporated milk
¼ cup grated Parmesan cheese

Directions

1. Cook noodles and drain. **2.** Combine other ingredients and heat. **3.** Pour on pasta and heat.

Pizza

"Pizza is the Italian dish that has become an American staple. Top your pie with spaghetti sauce, good mozzarella cheese, and vegetables including mushrooms, onions, tomatoes, and olives. My daughter loves it with pineapple. You can also top your pie with sausage, ground beef, Canadian bacon, or pepperoni." Linda

Ingredients

1 tsp. salt
5 lbs. flour
3 pkgs. yeast
1 egg

1 T. oil
Enough warm water to mix to correct consistency

Additions: red spaghetti sauce, Alfredo sauce, cheese, and toppings you like best.

Directions

1. Mix everything together until dough feels workable (not sticky). **2.** Knead for approximately 10 minutes, stretching it over itself to trap as much air as possible. **3.** Put dough in a warm spot and cover with a damp cloth. Leave it to double in bulk and knead again for about 15 minutes. Leave it to rise again. **4.** Knead one more time for 10 minutes and cut into 6 separate pieces. **5.** The five other pieces can be wrapped and frozen for five other pizzas. **6.** Roll out the dough on a floured board and put on a pizza pan. **7.** Spread with spaghetti sauce and top with cheese and toppings. **8.** Bake in a 400° oven until brown and bubbly.

Pork Tenderloin Roasted

"Pork roast is succulent and impressive. It is also versatile. You can cover it in savory spices, lay it on a bed of sauerkraut, and roast it slowly, or you can poke holes in it, stuff with garlic, surround with chopped and buttered red potatoes, and roast slowly, or you can marinate it in spices and maple syrup and roast it slowly with sweet potatoes. The key is roasting it slowly. The roast stays moist and whatever you are cooking with it drinks in the juices that emit during cooking." Linda

Ingredients
4–6 lb. pork tenderloin
1 bunch fresh marjoram
1 bunch fresh sage
5–6 cloves garlic
1 tsp. salt
Olive oil

Directions
1. Wash and pat dry all herbs. Remove large stems. **2.** In a blender or food processor, finely chop garlic, marjoram and sage with a little olive oil. **3.** Trim pork roast and coat with herb mixture. Refrigerate overnight for best flavor. **4.** Cook in a 350° oven for 30 minutes. **6.** Let stand for 10 minutes before slicing.

Variations
1. Cover the bottom of a roasting pan with a jar of sauerkraut that has been drained of half its juice. Put the tenderloin on top of the sauerkraut and roast.

2. Or marinate the roast overnight in maple syrup. Put salt, pepper, and garlic salt on the meat; then pour the syrup liberally over the roast because it will make a great sauce the next day. Cover and refrigerate. The next day, spray your pan with vegetable spray, so the sauce won't stick. Put your roast in the pan. Pour the marinade over it again and bake.

Pot Pie

"In those days when my world is not welcoming, pot pie is a wonderful retreat at mealtime. For years, I purchased frozen ones but this recipe is simple, and I can cook it with whatever is on hand. Should I be too busy to mix the suggested crust, I just dump the rest of the ingredients into a cooking dish and top with leftover mashed potatoes." Lael

Ingredients

½ cup milk
1 egg
1 cup biscuit mix
1⅔ cups left-over vegetables or 1, 15 oz. frozen or canned vegetables, thawed or drained
1 cup cooked chicken, beef, or pork, diced
10.5 oz. can condensed cream (mushroom, chicken, or celery) soup, undiluted, or 1½ cups gravy

Directions

1. Preheat oven to 350°. **2.** Mix vegetables, meat, and soup or gravy until moistened. **3.** Spread into a greased pie plate or casserole dish. **4.** In a small bowl, whisk the biscuit mix, milk, and egg until smooth. **5.** Pour over vegetable mixture. **6.** Bake for 30 minutes.

Variations

Instead of using biscuit mix to make a crust, layer flattened crescent roll dough on top of the vegetable and meat mixture and then bake. You could also use a pie crust that you make from scratch or buy in the frozen food section for below and on top of the filling.

Quiche Lorraine

"Ah, the treachery of cooking history! Despite the fact that this old recipe is named for the Lorraine region in France, its origin is German, and it also has English modifications. No wonder it is considered everybody's classic." Lael

"Quiche is wonderful for breakfast or brunch, of course, but when you add those green vegetables to it, it is also the perfect dinner food. Add a salad, and for those over twenty-one a great wine, and you will feel very French, even if quiche did begin in Germany." Linda

Ingredients

1, 9" single uncooked pie shell
6 slices bacon
3 eggs, beaten
1½ cups light cream
1½ cups shredded Swiss or Gruyere cheese
1 T. flour

Additions: ½ tsp. salt, ½ tsp. white pepper, 1 diced onion, ½ lb. of whatever you like—spinach, broccoli, mushrooms, sausage, or ham.

Directions

1. Preheat oven to 350°. Bake crust in preheated oven for 8 minutes or until a light brown. **2.** Reduce oven temperature to 325°. Brown bacon and remove from pan; crumble and set aside. **3.** In a large bowl, mix together eggs, cream and salt. Stir in bacon. In a separate bowl, toss cheese and flour together. Add cheese to egg mixture; stir well. **4.** Pour mixture into hot pastry shell. Bake for 35 to 40 minutes, or until knife inserted into center comes out clean. If necessary, cover edges of crust with foil to prevent burning. **5.** Let quiche cool for 10 minutes before serving.

Ranch Roast

"Anyone who comes into your home when this is simmering on the stove will angle for an invitation. Its aroma is that compelling and the taste is delicious. This works well in the crockpot, too." Linda

Ingredients

1 T. oil
1–5 lb. chuck roast
1, 16 oz. bottle of Catalina salad dressing
6 sliced potatoes
6 sliced carrots
6 sliced onions

Directions

1. Put oil and roast into a regular stew pot and brown roast on both sides. **2.** Remove roast from pot. Add ½ cup water to pan and mix with pan drippings. **3.** Put roast back in pot. **4.** Empty entire bottle of Catalina dressing into pot. Fill bottle with water and add to pot. Cover and cook over low heat for three hours. **5.** Layer vegetables on top of roast. **6.** Cover again and cook for another hour.

Red Flannel Hash

"Beets were a staple of my Maine childhood, and Red Flannel Hash, made with leftover roast beef, was a favorite dish. My husband, who hailed from Massachusetts, was raised with the same recipe except his family used salt codfish–then cheaper than roast beef but today more expensive. Their name for it was Cape Ann Turkey." Lael

Ingredients

- 4 cups cooked beef, chopped
- 4 cups boiled potatoes, chopped
- 4 cups boiled beets, chopped
- 1 small onion minced
- 1 cup cream
- 4 T. butter

Directions

1. Mix meat or fish and vegetables. Add enough cream to make them all stick together like hash should. **2.** Heat butter in fry pan, add hash and brown one side like an omelet. Then turn over and brown other side. **3.** Serve hot.

Variation

Boiled salt cod can be substituted for beef. If you go with fish, also use ¼ lb. salt pork cut into ¼" squares.

Salisbury Steak

"According to Wikipedia, this American stand-by was invented by Dr. James H. Salisbury (1823–1905), a New York state physician who was an early proponent of a low carb diet. Also know, however, that this recipe is excellent served with both noodles and mashed potatoes. Sorry, Doc!" Linda

Ingredients

1 lb. ground beef
1 cup breadcrumbs
1 beaten egg
¼ cup onion, chopped
10.5 oz. can condensed mushroom soup, undiluted
1½ cups mushrooms, sliced

Directions

1. Mix beef, breadcrumbs, beaten egg, onions and ¼ of the soup. Shape into 6 patties. **2.** Brown patties, remove from pan, and spoon off fat. **3.** Stir in remaining soup and mushrooms. **4.** Return patties to pan. Put heat on low, cover, and simmer for 20 minutes.

Salmon Pie or Peirok in Russian

"Also spelled Pirok and Perok, it always translates to 'Salmon Pie.' This still-popular recipe was introduced to Alaskan Aleuts by Russian fur hunters who enslaved them in the mid-1700s. Originally, it involved chopped hard-boiled eggs and shredded cabbage, neither of which was readily available in the Aleutian Islands. For that reason, this simpler version was preferred by my neighbors when I lived in Atka and Unalaska." Lael

Ingredients

1 pound (canned or fresh cooked) salmon, flaked
1 cup cooked rice
½ medium onion, grated
2 T. butter
5.5 oz. mushroom soup concentrate (half a can), with equal amount of water

Puff pastry, 2 refrigerator pie crusts or rolled-out Bisquick pie crust for top and bottom, allowing extra dough to drape over the edge

Directions

1. Preheat oven to 350°. **2.** Sauté in butter the onion until tender. **3.** Add fish, rice, and mixed soup or cream to sauté pan and heat. Add some juice from salmon if canned. **4.** Roll out pastry and fit bottom crust to deep-dish pie plate. **5.** Add filling. **6.** Add top crust, draping a small bit artistically over the sides. **7.** Bake for 45 minutes or until brown.

Variations

1. Heavy cream can be substituted for the mushroom soup mix. ½ small cabbage, cored and shredded, or two stalks of celery, chopped, may be sautéed with the onion until tender. **2.** Also a treat is the addition of 1 to 6 hard-boiled eggs, sliced and layered with pie filling.

Saucy Sirloin Burgers

"Save this recipe for a time when you find yourself on a hamburger budget for too long. It is easy to imagine the finished product is actually a neat little steak." Lael

Ingredients

1 lb. ground sirloin patties
3 tsp. beef bouillon
1 ½ cups hot water with 2 T. flour, mixed until no lumps

1 large onion, sliced
1, 4 oz. can mushroom pieces
Oil or butter in which to fry

Additions: 1 T. Worcestershire sauce, salt and pepper.

Directions

1. Coat each side of chopped sirloin patties with 3 T. flour. **2.** Heat oil or butter in skillet until hot. Add patties and brown on both sides. **3.** When brown, remove and pour off excess oil. Add floured water to the pan and stir in 3 tsp. beef-flavored bouillon until dissolved. **4.** Add sliced onion, mushroom pieces, and Worcestershire sauce. Stir sauce and then add patties. Cover and simmer gently for 25 minutes or until fork-tender.

Scotch Roast

"This recipe is surprisingly elegant, which is why my mother always served it when she felt like tricking us into thinking we were wealthy." Lael

Ingredients

4 lb. blade chuck roast
10.5 oz. can of condensed tomato soup, undiluted
1 cup barley, uncooked
1 ½ cups water
1 small onion, chopped
1 tsp. sugar

Additions: salt, pepper and parsley for seasoning.

Directions

1. Preheat heat oven to 250°. **2.** Season roast with salt and pepper. Then put in roasting pan. **3.** Mix remaining ingredients and pour over roast. **4.** Cover tightly and bake 2½ hours, turning roast over after first hour and a half, and stirring barley well. **5.** To serve, spoon barley mixture into deep platter and place sliced meat on top. Garnish with parsley, if desired.

Shellfish Steamed

"Once in a while, a large storm will toss a big bunch of quahog (also known as hard clams) on New England beaches. They are the biggest of the mussel family (about the size of cereal bowls) and really tough to open. So tough, in fact, a neighbor once gifted me with a bucket full of them after struggling all morning to open just a few dozen for himself. To his astonishment, I poured a bottle of wine in the bucket, capped it with tinfoil, steamed the critters open and made a banquet for us in about 10 minutes." Lael

Ingredients
1 medium onion, chopped
1 T. chopped garlic
2 T. butter
1 cup dry white wine
3 tomatoes peeled, seeded, and chopped
4 lbs. well-cleaned mussels or clams

Additions: Melted butter for dipping.

Directions
1. Sauté onion and garlic in butter until onion is transparent. **2.** Add white wine and tomatoes. Simmer 3 minutes. Add mussels. **3.** Cover and steam 5 to 8 minutes until opened. Remove mussels to warm plate. Reduce cooking liquid in pan over high heat until moderately thick and pour over mussels in serving dish.

Shepherd's Pie

"As I traveled throughout Ireland, I tasted a number of versions of Shepherd's Pie. Some I loved better than others. Though they all had the same basic ingredients, the spices and the meats (leftover beef, mutton, or lamb) varied.

"I learned along the way that originally the dish was called Cottage Pie and dated back to 1791 when the potato was first introduced to the Irish diet. It's said that the original crust was not made with mashed potatoes but with sliced potatoes laid in an overlapping pattern, like the roof of a cottage. Hence the name. The name Shepherd's Pie was coined in the 1870s and generally indicates the pie that includes mutton or lamb, though my favorite is still the version with beef." Linda

Ingredients

2 T. butter
2 cups cubed cooked lamb, beef, or chicken
1 large onion, chopped
2 T. flour
½ cup beef broth
2 cups seasoned mashed potatoes

Additions: 2 tsp. Worcestershire sauce, 2 stalks celery, diced, and ¾ cup chopped carrots, ¾ cup peas, ¾ cup tomatoes, and grated cheese for topping.

Directions

1. Preheat oven to 450°. **2.** Heat butter, meat, onion and other additions in large skillet until vegetables are tender, stirring often. Stir in flour. Gradually add beef broth. Cook until mixture boils, stirring constantly. Stir in Worcestershire sauce, if desired. **3.** If skillet is ovenproof, top with mashed potatoes and cheese. If not, put mixture in a baking pan and top with potatoes and cheese. **4.** Cook until top browns (about 10 minutes).

Sloppy Joes

"These sandwiches have long been an American favorite. Found in early 20th century cookbooks, they are, in fact, even more American than apple pie. Served on hamburger buns, crusty rolls or even toasted bread, they will always be a hit." Linda

Ingredients

2 lbs. ground chuck
1 large onion, chopped
2 cloves garlic, minced
½ cup ketchup
⅓ cup brown sugar, packed
3 T. soy sauce
14 oz. spaghetti sauce

Directions

1. In a large skillet, cook the beef, onion, and garlic over medium heat until meat is no longer pink; drain. Stir in spaghetti sauce, ketchup, brown sugar, and soy sauce. **2.** Bring to a boil. Reduce heat; cover and simmer for 15–20 minutes, stirring occasionally. **3.** Spoon about ½ cup meat mixture onto each bun.

Variation

1. Brown meat, onions, and garlic. **2.** Add 8 oz. bottle of taco sauce. **3.** Add 4 oz. can of drained green chilies and ¼ tsp. salt. **4.** Simmer 8–10 minutes. **5.** Spoon over crushed corn chips. **6.** Top with grated cheese.

Spaghetti Sauce

"This delightful dish is more than food to Italians, who call it 'gravy,' not sauce. Simmered all day on the stove tops of Italian mothers and grandmothers, it is credited with longevity and even satisfaction with life. The key to great gravy is subtle flavor.

"Spaghetti sauce can be used in five different dishes in one week. Pour it over any pasta and sprinkle with grated Parmesan or Romano cheese for a delicious side dish. Add sausage or pork ribs to the pot of sauce and cook for one hour more. Serve it with buttered noodles or rice. Simmer Italian meatballs in the sauce or cook chicken in the sauce for great cacciatore. For a great snack, heat some sauce and dip in some freshly made bread. You'll think you've gone to heaven, or at least to Italy." Linda

Ingredients

2 T. olive oil
1 lb. mild Italian sausage and/or 1 lb. pork bone
5 garlic cloves, peeled
½ cup tomato paste
3, 14½ oz. cans or fresh chopped tomatoes
Pasta (thick or angel hair)

Additions: fresh basil, oregano, salt and pepper

Directions

1. Heat olive oil in a large heavy pot (use a seasoned pot if you have one). **2.** Place the pork in the pot and brown until just about cooked. Transfer pork to plate. **3.** Do the same with the sausage and transfer to plate. Leave fat in pot. **4.** Add whole garlic cloves and sauté until tender. Put garlic on plate with meat. **5.** Stir in tomato paste until "saucy". **6.** Add tomatoes to the pot. **7.** Add basil, oregano, salt and pepper. **8.** Add the meats and garlic to the sauce and bring to a boil. Turn down to low and cook for about 1½ hours. Leave the sauce on low and remove all the meat. **9.** Cook pasta as directed but add both salt and vegetable oil to the water. **10.** Drain pasta.

Variations

1. Brown ground chuck with onions, garlic, and olive oil and add to sauce before pouring on pasta for spaghetti with meat sauce.

Spanish Rice

"This delicious dish has about as much to do with Spain as Arctic exploration, but it's a tasty basic that can be dressed up with exotic additions to serve as the main course. It is also incredibly cheap to produce at its simplest. So cheap, I swear that I could not have worked my way through college without it." Lael

Ingredients
4 T. butter
1 onion, chopped
2 cups cooked or instant rice

8 oz. can of tomato sauce
16 oz. can stewed tomatoes
Water if juice is lacking

Additions: ¼ cup chopped green pepper, ¼ cup chopped celery, and 1 cup cooked chicken, tuna fish, shrimp or hamburger, garlic salt, salt, and pepper.

Directions
1. Melt butter in large skillet and lightly brown onions. **2.** Add tomato sauce, canned tomatoes, rice and any extras you have included to dress up this dish. Add a bit of water if there is not enough juice. Simmer slowly until you are ready to serve.

Variation
1. Sauté onion and meat or seafood in butter. **2.** Add chopped green pepper. **3.** Add 1 cup washed, uncooked rice. **4.** Add 1, 16-oz. can of chopped tomatoes. **5.** Add spices. **6.** Cover and cook on low until liquid is absorbed.

Tortilla Wraps

"Once the mainstay in the Mexican diet only, tortillas have become the wrap of choice by everyone who loves easy eating. Cooks can fill them with scrambled eggs, bacon, or sausage, shredded cheese, and salsa for breakfast burritos to die for, can layer them with cold meats, sliced cheeses, and fresh chopped vegetables for delicious lunches and after-school snacks, and can stuff them with hot chili, sautéed meats, and stir-fried vegetables for hearty dinners. Remember, you can add hot/mild sauce, guacamole, and sour cream to any of the above for even more flavor." Linda

Ingredients

1 cup cooked chili
8 oz. canned corn
1 fresh tomato, chopped
1 green onion, chopped
½ cup shredded cheddar cheese
4 tortillas

Additions: chopped jalapeno, green or red peppers

Directions

1. Spread chili on tortillas. **2.** Spoon on corn, tomato, onion and peppers, if you have decided to add them. **3.** Sprinkle with cheese. **4.** Fold and warm in microwave.

Turkey à la King

"This exotic dish is credited to a number of famous hotel chefs, the most likely being William King who presided over the Bellevue Hotel in Philadelphia. The original version apparently included truffles, but even without them, it is excellent served with rice, pasta, mashed potatoes, puff pastry, or over toasted English muffins." Linda

Ingredients

- 1 white onion, diced
- 2 T. olive oil
- 3 T. pimento
- 10.5 oz. can condensed cream of mushroom soup, undiluted
- 1 can of milk or half & half, depending on how rich you want the dish to be
- 2 cups leftover turkey, chopped

Additions: diced green pepper, sautéed mushrooms

Directions

1. Sauté onions in olive oil and add diced pimento. **2.** Add mushroom soup to pan with one can of milk or half/half, and beat until sauce is smooth. **3.** Put in chopped turkey and mix until moistened. **4.** Cook mixture on low for 10 minutes. **5.** Pour into shells and serve.

Variations

Replace turkey with chicken or ham.

Veal Cutlets

*"Although my mother was raised on a dairy farm or perhaps **because she was**, she never served veal. In fact, I didn't even know the meat existed until at age seventeen when I joined a summer stock company in Livermore Falls, Maine, which had a diner famous for its cutlets. Smitten, I dined on them an average of five days a week for the whole three-month season. And I still favor this recipe over the most expensive steak. The secret to the appeal of this dish, however, is not my simple recipe but knowing a butcher you can trust."* Lael

Ingredients

4 veal cutlets, ½" thick
1 ½ cups bread or cracker crumbs
2 ½ T. grated Parmesan cheese
1 egg
2 T. water
Butter for browning

Additions: Garlic salt or minced garlic, ½ tsp. dried herbs including oregano, rosemary, savory, chervil, and mozzarella cheese. Serve with spaghetti sauce.

Directions

1. Preheat oven to 300° or use a frying pan if preferred. **2.** Rub cutlets with garlic salt or minced garlic. **3.** Mix crumbs with Parmesan cheese and spices. **4.** Beat egg with 2 T. water. **5.** Dip cutlets in egg mixture and then crumb mixture. **6.** Melt butter in frying pan and brown cutlets over low heat. **7.** Cover and continue cooking for 30 minutes or bake in oven for 50 minutes. **8.** Just before serving, add mozzarella cheese, if desired, and heat until it melts. Pouring on spaghetti sauce also adds flavor.

Welsh Rarebit

"Legend has it this recipe was developed by a Welsh rabbit hunter who came home empty-handed. Some of us still prefer it to rabbit meat. My mother always added a can of concentrated tomato soup, undiluted, and called her concoction 'Blushing Bunny' which were among the very first words in my vocabulary. She served it often, perhaps with an eye to her minuscule grocery budget, but also because my brother and I loved the concoction. We still do." Lael

Ingredients

8 oz. sharp cheddar cheese, shredded
¼ cup sour cream
2 tsp. Worcestershire sauce
½ tsp. dry mustard
4 slices or toast or equivalent servings of crackers (saltines)

Additions: dash of paprika and cayenne and/or one 10.5 oz. can of concentrated tomato soup, undiluted and/or ½ cup beer or ale.

Directions

1. Cook sour cream, Worcestershire sauce, dry mustard and beer or ale in a covered pot (use a double boiler if you have one) over very low heat until hot. **2.** Add cheese and stir until melted. Then add concentrated tomato soup if desired. **3.** Serve immediately over toast or crackers.

Gravy, Sauces, and Toppings

"Food cooked simply can be so very good, but food that is bathed in a delicious sauce is spectacular. It allows for multiple flavors to be enjoyed in one bite. It ensures bringing out the best in any dish, and it can cover a multitude of sins, so even if the dish isn't perfect, if it has a perfect sauce, you will still have a hit." Linda

Basil Pesto

"This versatile sauce can be used on any pasta, for dipping (bread and vegetables), and for spreading on vegetables or entrees that you want to be sumptuous." Linda

Ingredients
2 cups fresh basil leaves, chopped and loosely packed
2 T. garlic, chopped
½ cup toasted pine nuts (almonds and walnuts make a good substitute)
½ cup plus 2 T. olive oil
¾ cup freshly grated Parmesan cheese (plus ¼ cup for topping)
1 tsp. fresh lemon juice

Directions
1. Put garlic, pine nuts, oil, and basil into food processor and puree. Scrape the sides down to thoroughly blend. **2.** Add the cheese and lemon juice. Puree again. **3.** Cover and refrigerate. **4.** If adding to pasta, be sure pesto is room temperature and pasta is warm.

Variations
Herb Pesto—Increase to ⅔ cup olive oil and add 2 T. oregano, 1 T. rosemary, and ½ cup flat leaf parsley.
Sun-dried Tomato Pesto—Replace basil with 2–3 oz. pkg. sun-dried tomatoes and add ½ cup flat-leaf parsley.

Brown Gravy

"Often after sautéing or baking foods, lots of delicious bits or liquids are left at the bottom of the pan. Don't waste those morsels. Those luscious, full-flavored renderings can be the basis of a delicious roux that can be used to thicken liquids like soup or brown gravy." Linda

Ingredients
4 T. pan drippings and/or butter

6 T. flour

½ cup hot water

Directions
1. Mix flour, pan drippings, and hot water in a cup until completely smooth. 2. Add mixture to remainder of the drippings. Use a whisk to mix the gravy until smooth and thick.

Cheese Sauce

"When I was young, I was an athlete, a dancer, and a model through high school and college. I was so active that I didn't have to worry too much about calories, but even now when I am quite sure my metabolism has gone on hiatus and I do have to watch what I eat, I still cannot imagine giving up cheese. It is the perfect food in my opinion—creamy, flavorful, and the perfect addition to almost any recipe, so what might you do with a great cheese sauce? Pour it with pride. This one is perfect for fish, shrimp with lemon, and vegetables." Linda

Ingredients
2 T. water
2 T. flour
1 cup milk
½ cup Parmesan cheese
1 cup grated cheddar cheese
1 T. mustard, Dijon preferred

Additions: To top the sauce, sauté in 3 T. butter until brown, ¼ cup slivered almonds; then add 2 cups breadcrumbs to the pan and brown.

Directions
1. Preheat oven to 350°. **2.** In saucepan, add water to flour and mix until there are no lumps. **3.** Add milk and mustard; then mix in Parmesan cheese until smooth. **4.** Add cheddar cheese and pour over vegetables or casserole. **5.** Bake for 15 minutes.

Garlic Wine Sauce

"The French are known for their sauces made unbelievably delicious with butter and cream, and luscious on ham, fish, chicken, and vegetables. When French women were asked how they stayed slim on such a rich diet, they replied that they never denied themselves, but they only ate a few bites. Believe it or not, we can be satisfied with smaller portions.

"The flavor of sauces can be deepened with wine; red adds richness and white makes it a little fruity. When you add wine, let it cook down almost all the way. The alcohol cooks off, but the flavor remains." Linda

Ingredients

3 T. garlic, minced
3 T. shallots, minced
1 ½ cups brown chicken stock
½ cup red wine

3 T. butter, softened
½ tsp. salt and ½ tsp. black pepper

Directions

1. Combine the garlic, shallots, salt and pepper in a saucepan over high heat. **2.** Stir in the stock and the wine and bring to a boil. Cook over medium heat for 15 minutes. **3.** Swirl in the butter, remove from the heat, and continue to whisk in the butter until thoroughly incorporated.

Variation
Ingredients

¼ cup butter
¼ cup flour
1 ½ cups milk

1 cup light cream
1 egg yolk, beaten
¼ cup green onions in ¼" pieces

Directions

1. Melt butter in saucepan. Add onion (and green pepper) and cook until tender. **2.** Stir in flour and salt. **3.** Add 1 cup of milk and light cream all at once; cook until thickened, stirring constantly. **4.** Combine remaining ½ cup milk and egg yolk. To avoid curdling, stir a small amount of hot sauce into this mixture. Keep adding hot-to-cold until combined.

Hollandaise Sauce

"*Delicious on steak, vegetables, and a must over asparagus and Eggs Benedict, which is just a poached egg served on a slice of ham on an English muffin. There is no comparison to the pleasure of eating Hollandaise made from scratch. A double boiler will provide the gentle heat necessary to keep Hollandaise or Béarnaise sauce from curdling. Be careful not to add salt before cooking the yolks as it will cause curdling. If your sauce does curdle, strain out the solids and start anew with a warm egg yolk and 1 tsp. water. This also works for rewarming sauces that have been in the refrigerator.*" Lael

"*Always add cold liquids slowly to hot liquids to avoid curdling. The best guarantee is to put the cold liquid in a bowl. Keep adding hot liquid from the pot to it slowly. When the liquid is warm enough, pour it back into the pot of hot liquid.*" Linda

Ingredients
5 large egg yolks
½ tsp. salt
½ cup water

12 T. butter cut into slices
2 T. fresh lemon juice

Directions
1. Beat egg yolks with salt and water as you heat over very low heat in top of double boiler. **2.** When mixture is warm, add butter one slice at a time, blending in each piece before adding another. **3.** Once all butter has been added, remove from heat and stir in lemon juice. Serve immediately.

Horseradish Sauce

"This sauce is a simple but absolutely wonderful garnish for roast beef and a number of other meats." Lael

Ingredients
1 cup whipping cream
¼ cup creamed horseradish
   (more or less to taste)
1 tsp. salt
1 tsp. pepper
Minced garlic to taste

Directions
1. Whip cream until stiff. **2.** Add horseradish, garlic and seasonings.

Mustard Crème Sauce

"Serve this sauce with even the simplest poultry, beef, fish, and vegetables dishes, and they will be transformed." Linda

Ingredients
⅓ cup mustard,
   Dijon preferred
2 eggs
1 cup light cream
1 T. vinegar
¼ tsp. tarragon or dill weed

Directions
1. In a saucepan, beat all ingredients until smooth. **2.** Cook over low heat, stirring constantly until mixture thickens.

Newburg Sauce

"Sauces should enhance and complement the flavor of your dishes, not drown out what is being sauced. If you are serving a dish with the sauce already on, pour sparingly. Your guest can always add more. Be sure you fill a gravy boat with more sauce for the table. This sauce dresses up plain fish fillets and is delicious on toast, mashed potatoes, and vegetables." Linda

Ingredients
10.5 oz. can of condensed cream of shrimp soup, undiluted

¼ cup light cream

2 T. sherry

Additions: ¾ cup cooked shrimp

Directions
1. Blend all ingredients in saucepan and heat, stirring occasionally.

Tartar Sauce

"Don't ever attempt to fathom the history of this recipe or its name. Just take my word that the idea has been around for centuries and that this chunky sauce is a great accompaniment to any kind of fish." Lael

Ingredients
1 cup mayonnaise, "lite" preferred

¼ cup sour cream

2 T. finely chopped dill pickle

2 T. finely chopped onion

1 T. lemon juice

Dash of pepper

Directions
1. Mix ingredients and refrigerate before serving.

Rockport Red Sauce

"I live in the middle of Texas. When I moved here, people told us that it took four and one-half hours to get anywhere good and to go at night because there wasn't anything to see on the way. That has changed significantly during the last thirty years. There are now quaint towns, monuments, parks and shopping centers all along the way to any major city.

"When I think of Texas, however, the beach never leaps to mind and the ones along the southern coast are certainly not like the beaches of my youth. But Texas does have the bay and amazing lakes—huge, blue, and filled with fresh seafood. Rockport (where this sauce gets its name), Texas, is great town for both swimming and fishing. Overlooking Aransas Bay on the eastern coast, Rockport is known for the Texas Maritime Museum, the Fulton Mansion, which is on the National Register of Historic Places, and this sauce, which is delicious with shrimp and raw oysters." Linda

Ingredients
1 cup ketchup
3 T. lemon juice
1 T. horseradish
½ tsp. celery salt
½ tsp. hot pepper sauce

Directions
1. Mix ingredients and refrigerate before serving.

White Gravy

"Whether you are making chicken fried steak, biscuits, or a bowl of steamed vegetables, a white gravy can enhance flavor and turn simple fare into the sublime." Linda

Ingredients
5 slices bacon or ½ lb. sausage
¼ cup onion, diced
1 T. butter
4 T. flour
3 cups milk
½ tsp. salt and ¾ tsp. black pepper

Directions
1. Brown the bacon or the sausage in a large skillet, over medium-high heat. Remove from pan, cool on a paper towel to degrease, and then crumble. **2.** Add the butter and onions to the pan, and cook until onions are just brown. **3.** Turn the heat to low and add the flour. Cook about 3 minutes or until roux smells nutty. **4.** Whisk in the milk and pepper and bring to a boil over low heat, stirring often. **5.** Add the crumbled bacon or sausage.

Variation
Melt 4 T. butter in saucepan over low heat. Blend 4 T. flour, salt and pepper; cook until smooth and bubbly. Stir in 2½ cups milk. Heat to boiling on medium heat, stirring constantly.

Tips for Easier Entrees

1. In most grocery stores, you can buy all the best foods for you (vegetables, fruits, dairy, meats and fish) from the perimeter of the store. The foods on the aisles are the processed foods, the junk foods, and the most expensive offerings in the store.

2. Add sprigs of rosemary and oregano to rice, pasta and vegetable cooking water. Oregano has three to 20 times higher antioxidant activity than other herbs. Read Linda's book *Living Agelessly: Creating a Powerful Mid-life and Beyond* for complete information about all the amazing health benefits from including herbs and spices in your diet.

3. After you wash rice, add it to a heated pan that has a little melted butter. Mix thoroughly. Rice will not stick during or after cooking.

4. For fluffier, whiter rice, add one teaspoon of lemon juice per quart of water. To add extra flavor and nutrition to rice, cook it in liquid saved from cooking vegetables.

5. Add 1 T. of olive oil to the water in which you boil pasta or noodles. Noodles will not stick together. The oil also improves the flavor.

6. Marinate red meats in wine or balsamic vinegar to tenderize and flavor. For a juicier hamburger, add cold water to the beef before grilling (½ cup to 1 pound of meat). For tasty hamburgers that don't require onions and tomatoes later, mix in diced onions, tomato sauce, or V-8 juice and seasonings before shaping your patties.

7. Roll the package of bacon before opening. It separates more easily. Dip strips into cold water before frying and avoid "curly" bacon. Instead of frying the bacon, broil it and get rid of lots of fat. Line the bottom of the broiler with aluminum foil. When the pan cools, fold the foil and throw in trash. Pouring it down the drain can ruin your plumbing.

8. Deglazing is a technique used to create a base for making sauces. After you finish sautéing a food and removing excess fat, small bits of flavor-rich, browned food particles will be stuck to the pan. To loosen these bits, just add a small amount of liquid (broth, wine, stock, or lemon juice for example) to the pan and start stirring for a delicious "au jus". After searing steaks, deglaze your frying pan: add 2 T. of butter, a little white wine, and a splash of Grand Marnier. Serve sauce over steaks.

9. For jucier meat, do not carve for 10 minutes.

VEGETABLES AND SIDE DISHES

"Current healthy eating studies suggest that we should be getting four to six servings of fruits and vegetables a day. Doing so can be an endlessly creative endeavor. You can steam them with a little broth or butter, cream them with soup or cheese, or combine them with dressings to die for. One big salad per day can take care of the food requirement, and your imagination can supply the variety. Some recipes in this section can even be expanded to provide a fine main course." Linda

Acorn Squash

"Sailing halfway around the world with long stretches of open water and no refrigeration makes grocery acquisition and preservation a real challenge. That's when I really came to appreciate a tough little squash like acorn. It doesn't require any special handling, stays usable a long time and tastes divine, especially when other vegetables exist in nothing but memory. Despite my mother's Vermont roots, we never used maple syrup but brown sugar works just as well with this simple recipe." Lael

Ingredients

1 acorn squash, cut in half lengthwise
4 T. brown sugar
4 T. butter, softened
4 T. maple syrup
Kosher salt
Freshly ground black pepper

Directions

1. Preheat oven to 350°. **2.** Wash the exterior of the squash and cut in half lengthwise. **3.** Discard the seeds and stringy pulp from the squash cavity. **4.** In a small mixing bowl, combine the brown sugar, butter, syrup, and salt and pepper to taste. Rub the squash cavities and coat sides of the squash with the butter mixture. Pour the remainder of the sauce evenly into the cavities. **5.** Place the squash on a baking sheet, cut side up. **6.** Bake in the preheated oven for about 1 hour until the squash is tender when pierced with a fork.

Savory Squash

"Savory or sweet, squash is one of the most hardy and versatile vegetables. Though rich in nutrients, it has a subtle flavor that allows for absorbing all that is added, so feel free to sprinkle on basil, dill or parsley with salt and pepper. Use garlic and onions liberally and get creative with cheese. Though Parmesan is featured, try cheddar or mozzarella." Linda

Ingredients

1 acorn squash, cut in ½ lengthwise
2 T. olive oil
½ tsp. Kosher salt
½ tsp. freshly ground black pepper
¼ cup grated Parmesan (1 oz.)

Directions

1. Heat the oven (with oven rack in the middle) to 350°. **2.** Spray a sheet pan with cooking spray. Using your chef's knife, shave a thin piece from the side of the squash to prevent it from rolling when you halve it. **3.** Trim the ends of the squash and cut it in half (lengthwise) from stem to opposite end. **4.** Scoop out the seeds and pulp. Slice into ¾" thick half-moons. **5.** On the pan, drizzle the squash with the oil and rub to coat evenly. **6.** Season with ¼ tsp. salt, ¼ tsp. pepper and sprinkle with the ¼ cup Parmesan cheese. **7.** Turn the squash over and repeat with the remaining salt, pepper and Parmesan cheese. **8.** Roast, without turning, until the squash is golden brown and tender, 35 to 40 minutes.

Asparagus

"The main thing I recall about my first trip to Switzerland is that I found myself in an open air market that was selling the most beautiful asparagus I'd ever seen, but at the heinous price of $8 for a small bunch. Having just traveled from California where I was used to buying it for about $3 for a good sized bouquet, I was appalled, but the shock made me appreciate that princely vegetable. At its freshest, cooked with care, I decided asparagus might well be considered priceless." *Lael*

"My first introduction to asparagus was from a can—limp, lackluster, and even a little sickening since it had been cooked to death. There is nothing like fresh asparagus steamed lightly, spritzed with olive oil and sprinkled with garlic salt and fresh ground pepper." *Linda*

Ingredients

Asparagus, 1 bunch, chopped into 1" pieces
2 T. butter
1 pint heavy cream
½ cup fresh grated Parmesan cheese
1 clove garlic, thinly sliced

Directions

1. Wash and chop asparagus. Be sure to cut off and discard hard or discolored portion at the end of the stalk. **2.** Sauté garlic and asparagus in slightly browned butter. **3.** Add cream and then cheese. Stir until thickened.

Baked Beans

"This is a staple of the Northeast because it is cheap, super easy to prepare, and saves money when the cook stove is also used for heat. Traditionally cooked in an earthen pot with a heavy cover, baked beans were served on Saturday nights with corn bread or brown bread, and honey or butter." Lael

Ingredients

2 cup dry beans (pea, kidney, great northern, yellow-eyed or small white)
1 onion small, peeled
¼ lb. salt pork with rind
¼ cup molasses
½ heaping tsp. dry mustard
Water

Substitution: Vermonters often use maple syrup instead of molasses. Some add a bit of brown sugar or sorghum sugar. Some diners demand ketchup on the finished product and some like to add mustard and relish to the mix.

Directions

1. Soak beans overnight in cold water. Drain the next morning. 2. Cover beans with water in a saucepan and simmer until skins burst (about 10 minutes). 3. Remove from heat and drain. 4. Place onion in bottom of an oven-worthy bean pot, and cover with drained beans. 5. Cut through pork rind about ½" deep every ¾" and bury, rind up. 6. Mix molasses, mustard and 2 cups of boiling water and pour over beans and pork. Add more boiling water to cover, if necessary. 7. Bake 4–6 hours or more, covered, in a 300° oven, or cook in a covered crockpot on low, adding boiling water to cover each hour. Then one hour before beans are done, remove cover and continue cooking but add no more water. (If using an oven, pull salt pork to the top, so it will brown. If using crockpot, remove salt pork when beans are done and brown rind under broiler). 8. Put a piece of salt pork in each serving.

Note: The secret to great baked beans is being very careful to add water until that last hour and to remove the cover for that last hour of cooking.

Corn Bake

"Corn bakes are at least as popular as square dancing in corn country and there are a zillion ways to execute one for a crowd like your family reunion. Just go on the Internet and plug in 'corn on the cob for a crowd,' and you'll discover how to do it in a big picnic cooler with boiling water, over a campfire or maybe in your electric dishwasher. But if you don't need to go grandiose, take a careful look at the recipe that follows. It works just fine!" Lael

Ingredients

5 ears fresh corn or 1 pkg. frozen corn kernels
½ cup breadcrumbs
1 tsp. sugar

2 eggs, beaten lightly
½ cup milk
Butter

Directions

1. Preheat oven to 350°. **2.** Cut corn off cob, or thaw frozen corn. Mix with breadcrumbs and sugar. **3.** Stir milk into beaten eggs; add corn mixture, place in well-buttered baking dish and dot with butter. **4.** Bake 40 minutes.

Eggplant Baked

"I love eggplant in its every presentation—fried in olive oil after being dipped in egg and then breadcrumbs, baked between layers of red sauce and mozzarella cheese, smothered by layers of sliced onion, chopped tomatoes, and sautéed ground beef or lamb chops, or mashed with garlic and olive oil and served on red leaf lettuce with pita bread or pita chips for dipping.

"Most eggplants can be eaten with their skin. The larger ones and those that are whiter in color are sometimes tough. To remove their skin, you can peel them before cutting or if you are baking them, you can scoop out the flesh once it is cooked. If baking whole, be sure to pierce the eggplant several times with a fork to allow steam to escape.

"To tenderize the flesh and reduce its naturally bitter taste, sweat the eggplant by salting it. After cutting the eggplant into the desired size and shape, sprinkle it with salt and allow it to rest for about 60 minutes. Then rinse thoroughly to remove salt and the water it pulls out of the flesh. Then pat dry." Linda

Ingredients

1 large eggplant, washed
1 large garlic clove, cut in slivers
¼ cup olive oil

2 T. fresh lemon juice
1 T. oregano
½ tsp. ground cumin

Directions

1. Preheat oven to 400°. **2.** Cut slits in eggplant with knife tip and insert garlic sliver in each slit. **3.** Bake until tender, for about 1 hour. **4.** Cool slightly, cut in half and cool again. **5.** Scrape eggplant pulp from skin into colander and let drain. **6.** Transfer eggplant to processor and add oil, lemon juice, and spices. **7.** Puree to desired consistency. Add salt and pepper to taste. **8.** Cover and refrigerate. Can be made a day ahead. **9.** Serve with pita bread.

Eggplant Parmigiana

"Having been born in New England eight decades ago, I was late to hear about eggplant and even slower to appreciate it. It acts like a sponge in sucking up any oil in which you attempt to cook it, and its blandness was a bit of a shock to someone brought up on beets and cabbage. However, all its down points become plusses when you find a recipe that exploits its subtleties and matches it with a suitable sauce." Lael

Ingredients

2–3 large eggplants, sliced in ¼" rounds
6 eggs, beaten in one bowl
Breadcrumbs in another bowl

1.5 lbs. mozzarella, sliced about ⅛" thick
Parmesan cheese
Spaghetti sauce (recipe in Index)

Directions

1. Preheat oven to 350°. **2.** Salt each eggplant round on both sides; let set about 15–20 minutes. When moisture forms, rinse and blot thoroughly with paper towels. (This process removes bitterness.) **3.** Dip eggplant rounds in eggs, then in breadcrumbs and fry in shallow oil in a skillet. They will cook quickly since they are not thick. Cool on paper towels to absorb any oil. **4.** Assemble in a large baking dish: thin layer of sauce, single layer of eggplant, and a piece of mozzarella. Add another piece of eggplant, thin layer of spaghetti sauce, and cheese. If the dish is deep enough, repeat the same process. **5.** Top with another layer of sauce and grated Parmesan cheese. **6.** Bake for 1 hour.

Fried Green Tomatoes

"This dish was made famous by the movie of the same name. While the movie was about a lot more than cooking, this delicious comfort food had a starring role. As an isolated Yankee, I'd never heard of the dish until that movie appeared, but I hastened to get updated. This classic recipe is worth a try." Lael

Ingredients
4 green (not ripened) tomatoes
2 eggs, beaten
Flour to coat
Salt
Oil for frying

Directions
1. Slice tomatoes in rounds about ³⁄₈" thick, season with salt, and then dip in egg and flour to coat. **2.** Fry in shallow oil, doing one side at a time, or drop into deep fat to cook as you would French fried potatoes.

Fried Okra

"Many who haven't grown up with this southern staple find okra a bit slimy to the tongue, especially if stewed or sautéed. However, fried okra has become almost as popular as French fries in some southern fast food chains. If you think you don't like it, this recipe might change your mind." Lael

Ingredients
4 cups young okra, stems cut off
Boiling water to cover
Salt and pepper
3 cups corn meal
Oil for frying

Directions
1. Barely cover okra with boiling water and boil covered for 5 minutes. Drain and dry between towels. **2.** Sprinkle with salt and pepper and then dip in corn meal until well covered. **3.** Fry in shallow oil one side at a time or drop into deep fat to cook as you would French fried potatoes.

Grits

"I was well beyond the age of consent when I first encountered this southern staple. It is, however, a simple favorite that will make do as a meal if served with cooked greens or salad." Lael

Ingredients
1 cup grits, uncooked
2 cups grated cheddar cheese
2 eggs beaten
1/8 tsp. cayenne pepper
Paprika

Directions
1. Heat oven to 375°. **2.** Cook grits according to pkg. directions. **3.** Stir in 1½ cups cheese. Then add eggs and pepper, mixing well. Top with rest of cheese and sprinkle with paprika. **4.** Bake for 20 minutes.

Mashed Potatoes

"How to prepare this true comfort food varies from region to region and family to family, and though I don't think anyone's gone to war about it, consistency can be a touchy subject. My family loves chunky mashed potatoes with lots of flavor, so I am a big fan of cream, butter, and lots of garlic. Needless to say, I don't make it often or we'd all need cholesterol medication. I do also love the milk and chicken broth substitutions." Linda

"Mine always have unsightly lumps. All I had to do is convince my kin that lumps are our family tradition (which they sure as heck are) to stifle criticism." Lael

Ingredients

1 ½ lbs. potatoes, peeled and cut lengthwise into quarters
½ tsp. salt
½ cup light cream
¼ stick butter
1 T. milk (or more)
Salt and Pepper

Directions

1. Place peeled and cut potatoes into a medium saucepan. Add cold water (for more even cooking) to the pan until the potatoes are covered by at least an inch. Add ½ tsp. salt to the water. Turn the heat to high and bring to a boil. **2.** Reduce the heat to low to maintain a simmer, and cover. Cook for 15 to 20 minutes or until you can pierce the potatoes with a fork. **3.** While the potatoes are cooking, melt the butter and warm the cream. You can heat them together in a pan on the stove or in the microwave. **4.** When the potatoes are done, drain the water and place the steaming hot potatoes into a large bowl. Pour the heated cream and melted butter over the potatoes. **5.** Mash the potatoes with a potato masher. Then use a big wooden spoon (a metal spoon might bend) to beat further. Add milk and beat the mashed potatoes until desired smoothness is achieved. Don't over-beat the potatoes or mash the potatoes in a mixer or they will end up gluey.

Onion Rings in the Bag

"This recipe is so simple I always feel as if I'm cheating when I start shaking up the ingredients in a paper or plastic bag. However, the results are just as good as if I'd labored longer at the task, and how I love to eat them." Lael

Ingredients
2 big onions, sliced in rings
2 cups biscuit mix
3 cups milk

3 cups cooking oil or more for deep frying
Seasoning of your choice

Directions
1. Fill a bag with biscuit mix and seasonings of your choice. **2.** Heat oil in pan. **3.** Dip onion rings in milk, drain, and then drop into bag and shake until each is well covered. **4.** Fry in hot oil until golden brown and drain.

Potato Pancakes

"Where did the idea come from? Just about every nationality that ever encountered the potato has its own variation, and all of them are wonderful. Try the classic below." Lael

Ingredients
2 cups stiff mashed potatoes
1 egg, beaten
1 T. onion, minced

Flour to coat
Butter for frying

Directions
1. Stir egg and onion into mashed potatoes. Form patties and dip in flour. **2.** Fry in heated butter until golden.

Potatoes Parmesan

"Tired of fries? Tired of baked potatoes with sour cream and cheese? Here is an idea that will keep you from purchasing potato chips for at least a week. Dare I say it—this might actually be better for you?" Lael

Ingredients
6 potatoes
¼ cup butter
1 cup grated Parmesan cheese
1 tsp. garlic salt
1 tsp. pepper
1 tsp. parsley flakes

Directions
1. Preheat oven to 350°. **2.** Wash potatoes and cut in half. **3.** Poke cut side with a fork and dip in butter. **4.** Then dip in Parmesan cheese and spice mixture. **5.** Bake for 1½ hours.

Variation: Dill Potatoes
1. Cut in quarters small red potatoes and boil until fork tender. **2.** Drain potatoes and add butter, garlic salt, and dill weed to taste.

Potatoes Scalloped

"This recipe was a family staple, but I hadn't tried it in years when nostalgia recently overcame me. To my surprise, it is more delicious than I had remembered it, and I've come to think of it as a meal in itself on days when I'm feeling vegetarian." Lael

Ingredients

¼ cup butter plus enough to grease baking dish
3 T. flour
2 cups milk or light cream

4 cups thinly sliced potatoes
½ cup shredded cheese
1 small onion, thinly sliced in rings

Additions: ham or chipped beef and a sprinkle of paprika.

Directions

1. Preheat oven to 350° and butter baking dish. **2.** Melt butter in saucepan over medium heat and stir in flour until smooth. Gradually add milk and cook until mixture boils, stirring constantly. **3.** Layer half the potatoes, half the onion (separated into individual rings) and meat, if desired, in the baking dish. Top with sauce and repeat. Sprinkle with paprika. **4.** Bake covered for 1 hour. Then uncover and bake 15 minutes more or until potatoes are tender. **5.** Sprinkle with the cheese, return it to the oven and bake until cheese is melted.

Potatoes, Twice Baked

"Though this recipe is a bit more complicated than "once baked" spuds, they are worth the effort, and I still crave them." Lael

Ingredients

4 potatoes, washed
1 cup grated cheese (Swiss, Gruyere, cheddar, or jack)
2 eggs
5 T. heavy cream
1 tsp. salt
½ cup herbed butter (recipe in Index)

Directions

1. Heat oven to 375°. **2.** Bake potatoes. Cool and cut in half. **3.** Scoop out flesh and put into bowl. **4.** Place potato skins on cookie sheet and then into the oven to get crisp while putting filling together. **5.** Mash potato flesh. Add butter, cheese, cream, egg yolks, salt and beat until smooth. **6.** Whip egg whites until soft peaks form and fold into potato mixture. **7.** Mound potato into skins and put back into the oven for 20 to 25 minutes. The filling crust should be golden brown.

Sweet Potatoes California

"Lots of states grow sweet potatoes, but the California approach to cooking them is different. True, this technique may have been stolen from Hawaii. But let's not quibble. Just try it." Lael

Ingredients
6 large sweet potatoes, peeled
3 oranges
½ lb. butter
1 cup brown sugar

1 ½ tsp. cinnamon
1 cup unsweetened pineapple with juice

Directions
1. Preheat oven to 350°. **2.** Peel potatoes and slice or chop. **3.** Grate the rind of one orange. **4.** Peel oranges and section. **5.** Arrange potato and orange slices in layers in a buttered baking dish, dotting each layer with butter and sprinkling with sugar, cinnamon, and grated orange rind. **6.** Cover and bake for one hour.

Rice Re-do

"There is nothing as sad looking and unappetizing as the cold meats, hardened pastas, and limp vegetables that just one day before were luscious offerings. Don't toss those leftovers into the trash. With just a little effort, you can reinvent them into a new dish that is just as satisfying—maybe even better. Because the leftovers have had a chance to soak in the spices and dressings, they can be the tastiest part of another dish." Linda

Ingredients

1 cup cooked rice
2 T. olive oil
1 small red onion, chopped
1 garlic clove, minced
2 stalks of celery, chopped on an angle
¼ cup chicken broth or 1 bouillon cube and ¼ cup water

Additions: chopped green or red peppers, halved cherry tomatoes, green beans, pea pods, chopped chicken or turkey, and ¼ tsp. of basil, dill, thyme, or rosemary, and seasoned salt and pepper.

Directions

1. In olive oil, sauté garlic clove and red onion until softened. **2.** Add celery (and/or other suggested vegetables). **3.** Season vegetables with spices, salt and pepper. **4.** Add rice and chicken broth. **5.** Cover pan and cook until rice is hot.

Rice Pilaf

"This dish is a staple in the diet of Armenians. I know because my mother and my grandmother before her served it every Sunday when the entire family (aunts, uncles, and a bevy of young cousins) gathered for a variety of delicacies that are still unrivaled in my mind, though I may be just a little prejudiced.

"Pilaf is the perfect complement to shish kebab, yogurt, and dolma (stuffed vegetables of every sort). Actually, pilaf is the perfect complement to any entree—chicken, fish, or other beef dishes. Try it. You may never make rice any other way again!" *Linda*

Ingredients

¼ cup butter
½ cup skinny noodles (1" long and very thin), mini spaghetti, or Fideo
1 cup long grain rice (Uncle Ben's Unconverted is my favorite)
2 cups hot water
6 chicken bouillon cubes

Directions

1. Wash rice thoroughly under hot water to remove excess starch.
2. Sauté noodles in butter until brown.
3. Add rice to butter and noodles, and mix until rice is coated to avoid sticking.
4. Add hot water and bouillon cubes.
5. Cover and cook on low for 20 minutes or until all liquid is absorbed.

Spinach Italian

"This recipe is beautiful in its simplicity and will amaze you in its fresh, wonderful goodness. It really is an Italian treasure." Lael

"Spinach is a favorite of mine. For many years, though, I cooked it only one way—steamed it, squeezed out all water, and added it to sautéed onions. Then I cracked two eggs on the top and, with a fork, broke and swirled the eggs so they were mixed and covered the spinach. I covered the pan and let the steam cook the eggs. It is delicious, but Lael's recipe is so good, that I now alternate. I particularly love sprinkling the cooked spinach with Parmesan cheese. It is simple and wonderful." Linda

Ingredients

4 cups fresh spinach, washed
4 T. olive oil
1 clove garlic or more, chopped

Possible toppings: Cooked chicken or shrimp, and/or feta cheese if desired, or sprinkle with Parmesan cheese. The juice of a lemon also adds zest.

Directions

1. Heat oil in large frying pan. Sauté garlic. **2.** Remove pan from fire and drop in spinach. Cover and set on medium heat 6 minutes, stirring occasionally. **3.** If desired, add juice of lemon, feta or Parmesan cheese, and chicken or shrimp and heat through just before serving.

Squash Casserole

"When you or your friendly neighbor are growing squash and it comes into season, you can find yourself inundated with some thin-skinned varieties that don't keep very long. Challenged by the amount you will need to use quickly, you'll make squash muffins and even experiment with squash cake. I developed a decent recipe for zucchini pizza—slice the 'zuc" in two pieces, layer it with pizza sauce plus all the toppings and bake it as if it was the real thing. The recipe below is a different approach that I suspect you will grow fond of." Lael

Ingredients

3 squash, acorn or summer squash preferred, peeled
⅛ cup butter
1 onion, chopped
6 celery stalks, peeled and chopped
2 beaten eggs
2 cups cheddar cheese, shredded

Additions: Ritz crackers, crumbled

Directions

1. Boil squash for 30 minutes and mash. **2.** Preheat oven to 350°. **3.** Melt butter and sauté onions and celery. **4.** Add squash to mixture. **5.** Mix in egg and cheese. **6.** Crumble Ritz crackers and sprinkle on as topping, if desired. **7.** Bake for 30 minutes.

Variation

Slice zucchini and yellow squash into ¼" rounds. Layer the bottom of a greased baking dish with zucchini sprinkled with salt, pepper and basil, then put a layer of yellow squash, add spices and cover with shredded cheddar cheese, put another layer of spiced zucchini, another layer of spiced yellow squash, another layer of cheese and a layer of crushed Ritz crackers. Bake for 1 hour at 350°.

Stir-Fried Veggies

"I've gotten in the habit of keeping a big bag of frozen vegetables handy so I can make stir-fry with ease. It's less work than chopping up ingredients for a salad and if you add beef, chicken or seafood, you've taken care of your protein too." Lael

Ingredients

2 T. oil (olive oil or peanut oil for unique flavor)
1 clove of garlic, chopped
1 small slice of fresh ginger (or ½ tsp. ground)
1 tsp. fresh or dried herbs, chopped (parsley or basil)
2 T. soy sauce

4 cups thinly sliced vegetables (any firm vegetable sliced thin can be stir-fried) carrots, cabbage, green, red or yellow peppers, celery, asparagus, turnips, snow-peas, broccoli, bok choy, zucchini, squash, cauliflower, mushrooms, onions (any kind).

Additions: ½ tsp. salt, ½ tsp. pepper

Directions

1. Place 2 tsp. oil in 10" skillet or wok. Add garlic and ginger to the oil. Stir to season oil with garlic and ginger on medium high heat.
2. Toss thin-sliced veggies into oil and stir to coat all vegetables. Continue to stir every 10–20 seconds.
3. Add seasonings.
4. Stir-fry until vegetables get a little limp but still firm.

Variation

To make a glaze, add ⅓ cup water blended with 1 T. soy sauce and 1 tsp. of cornstarch to pan of stir fried veggies. Stir until vegetables are coated.

String Beans Almandine

"Yes, the Thanksgiving green bean recipe with onion rings on the can is loved. But consider this more sophisticated approach to serve to house guests who may be more discerning." *Lael*

"Now, Lael is making this recipe sound a little more pompous than it is. I actually threw this together because I had drop-in guests and only this in the freezer to make for the vegetable dish. Because it is so delicious and so easy, I now keep string beans in my freezer all the time. And if you serve it in a beautiful dish, it is even more impressive." *Linda*

Ingredients

1 bag frozen string beans
¼ stick butter, browned slightly for better flavor
¼ cup slivered almonds
½ onion, sliced thin
1 tsp. garlic salt
½ tsp. salt

Directions

1. Sauté almonds in a pat of butter just until brown. Add salt and stir. **2.** Add remainder of butter and sauté onions until translucent (about 5 minutes). Add garlic salt and stir. **3.** Steam string beans just until bright green. Drain. **4.** Add string beans to almonds and onions and mix well. Serve immediately.

Succotash

"This recipe comes down to us from our Pilgrim Fathers who got it from the Indians. The latter, not being dairymen, used water instead of cream and butter, but these ingredients do add. Be careful not to cook this dish too much, and watch your waistline." Lael

Ingredients

2½ cups baby lima beans, shelled (fresh or frozen)
1 cup water or more

3 ears of corn or 1¼ cup frozen corn kernels
1 T. butter
¼ cup heavy cream

Additions: meat or fish.

Directions

1. Heat beans in 1 inch of water, bringing it to a boil and then reducing heat to low, and simmering for 20 minutes or until beans are tender. 2. Cut corn from cob with a sharp knife and then scrape pulp from cob with dull side of knife. 3. Add corn and butter to beans and continue to simmer for 5 minutes. Stir in cream and heat through.

Variation

Sixteen ounces uncooked (or frozen) baby lima beans boiled in salted water until tender and drained, 14 oz. can corn, drained, and ⅛ cup butter, salt and pepper. Mix together and serve.

Turkey Stuffing, stove top

"Though a moist turkey was always the star on the holiday table, the costar was always my mom's stove top stuffing. Unlike the fare you create from boxes on grocery store shelves, her stuffing was moist, not one big glob, textured and not mushy, spicy and not bland. Often, most of it never made it to the table because every time folks passed the pan, they stole 'just one more bite.'" Linda

"Linda could have easily listed her stuffing recipe under entrees, because although it features veggies along with the bread and giblets, I occasionally enjoy it as a main course. I just add a salad." Lael

Ingredients

Giblets, the turkey's liver, heart, and gizzard, minced
1 stick butter
1 onion, chopped
1 can dried celery flakes
2 T. rubbed sage
2 tsp. thyme leaves
6 slices of whole wheat bread, dampened with water and chopped into ¾" squares

Additions: Salt and fresh pepper, 4 celery stalks, peeled and chopped, chopped mushrooms

Directions

1. Remove giblets from turkey cavity; rinse and mince. **2.** Melt butter until just brown in a large skillet. **3.** Sauté onions and celery. **4.** Add giblets, salt and pepper, and cook until brown, stirring constantly. **5.** Add celery flakes, sage, and thyme and stir in. **6.** Add dampened bread and stir until well coated. If dry, sprinkle on more water or chicken broth. **7.** Cook for 15 minutes over low heat, stirring occasionally.

Chicken Stuffing, in the bird

"I never stuff my turkey. It absorbs the juices, dries out the bird and makes a mush of the stuffing. Because it takes far less time to roast a chicken and there are fruits in this recipe, the stuffing is flavorful and the chicken is moist." Linda

Ingredients

1 cup celery, chopped and sautéed in ¼ cup butter
½ cup chopped pecans or hazelnuts
½ cup dried cranberries or ½ cup chopped prunes
6 slices of bread, cubed and moistened with chicken broth
½ tsp. each sage and thyme
Salt and pepper to taste

Directions

1. Cook celery and onion in butter in a small saucepan until tender. Remove from heat. **2.** Stir in sage, thyme, salt and pepper. **3.** Place dry bread cubes in a mixing bowl. Add celery mixture and nuts. **4.** Add cranberries or prunes and chicken broth, tossing to moisten. **5.** Prepare poultry—clean out cavity, wash bird in salty water, rinse thoroughly. Stuff cavity, butter chicken skin and sprinkle with seasoned salt. **6.** The internal temperature of stuffing should reach 165°. Do not overcook as stuffing can suck the bird dry.

Wild Rice

"This expensive grain is not actually rice but comes from a grass that produces look-alike seeds that were much enjoyed by early Great Lakes Indian tribes. It's an expensive dish, but well worth the investment for special occasions." Lael

Ingredients

1 cup raw wild rice
¼ cup butter
1 stalk celery, diced

2 cups mushrooms, sliced
2 cups chicken broth
½ cup almonds

Additions: 2 green onions, sliced thin and/or ¼ tsp. oregano leaves and ¼ tsp. thyme. To make this a main course, cook ½ pound ground pork sausage to add along with almonds.

Directions

1. Wash rice in warm (not hot) water and drain. **2.** In large saucepan melt butter, add celery and green onions and cook until tender. Then stir in mushrooms with crushed spices and cook just one minute more. **3.** Add broth and rice; bring to a boil. Lower heat and simmer covered about 45 minutes until rice is tender and all liquid is absorbed. **4.** Stir in almonds and sausage, if desired.

Zucchini Soufflé

Oh, Zucs! In season, I'm often up to my knees in them and find it a mixed blessing. This is one way to turn them into a substantial meal that everyone can enjoy." Lael

Ingredients
4 large zucchini, peeled and chopped
¼ cup olive oil
2 garlic cloves, crushed
2 medium sized onions, chopped
⅛ cup lemon juice
6 eggs, beaten

Additions: 1 tsp. salt, 1 tsp. pepper, 1 cup shredded cheddar cheese.

Directions
1. Preheat oven to 350°. **2.** Steam zucchini for ten minutes. **3.** Heat the oil. Sauté the onion and garlic. **4.** Add the steamed zucchini, lemon juice, and beaten eggs. **5.** If you're going to add other spices and cheese, this is the time. **6.** Bake in a soufflé dish for 45 minutes.

Tips for Dealing with Vegetables

1. The food value to the brain from vegetables and fruits is shockingly higher than anything else you can put on your plate.
2. Buy vegetables and fruits that are in season. They are generally less expensive, healthier and tastier.
3. Microwave garlic cloves for 15 seconds and the skins come right off.
4. When mincing garlic, sprinkle on a little salt so the pieces won't stick to your knife or cutting board.
5. To keep cauliflower white while cooking, add a little milk to the water. When boiling or steaming cauliflower, beets, or other vegetables, add a teaspoon or two of white distilled vinegar to the water to help them keep their color. The vinegar will improve their taste and reduce gassy elements. This also works when cooking beans and bean dishes.
6. Avoid frying foods when you can. When you want to sauté dishes, heat the frying or sautéing pan to medium heat before adding butter or oil. Not even eggs will stick. Sautéing is a quick and easy way to cook vegetables with relatively little oil. Sautéed vegetables retain their vitamins and minerals, as well as their taste and color. This method is best suited for tender vegetables including asparagus, baby artichokes, snow peas, sweet peppers, onions, and mushrooms. Cut vegetables into bite-sized pieces so they can cook all the way through quickly. Cooking time depends on the desired tenderness.
7. Always use the best knife for cutting vegetables—a paring knife, a chef knife for slicing and dicing. A serrated-edge knife, also known as a bread knife, is great for slicing tomatoes.
8. Many recipes call for a dice cut. Dicing creates a cube shape that is great for even cooking. To create large dice, best for braising or stewing, slice about ¾" apart, then turn and repeat. Medium dice, best for roasting or broiling, are ½", while small dice are ¼" and best for sautéing and soups.
9. Three types of matchstick cuts add interest to a dish and a pretty presentation. Start with a 2½" stick, and then cut into various thicknesses. A batonnet cut is ½" wide and best for roasting root vegetables. Alumette, at a ¼" wide, is best for faster cooking methods like steaming or sautéing. A julienne cut, ⅛" x ⅛", is the most common and is often used for carrots, celery, peppers, onions, and string potatoes.

DESSERTS

"Desserts have been dubbed the culprit for obesity, but the truth is that if you indulge in moderation, you can have your cake and eat it too!" Linda

Apple Brown Betty

"*New England has wonderful apples and if you store them in a cool place, they'll last pretty much through the winter. For these reasons, I have a huge collection of apple recipes but this is my very favorite. Served hot or with a simple hard sauce (butter with sugar mashed in and a dash of vanilla), whipped cream or ice cream, it is my idea of a dessert made in heaven.*" Lael

Ingredients

6 cups apples, pared, sliced, and cored
1 ½ T. lemon juice
2 cups breadcrumbs
¼ cup melted butter, with additional to grease pan
½ cup sugar, white or brown
½ cup water

Additions: 1 T. grated lemon rind, ½ tsp. nutmeg or mace, and/or 1 tsp. cinnamon. Whipped cream or hard sauce make good toppings for this dish.

Directions

1. Preheat oven to 375°. **2.** Combine crumbs and butter with lemon rind and spices and arrange ⅓ of mixture in the bottom of a greased casserole dish. **3.** Cover with half the apples. **4.** Combine sugar and remaining ingredients and use half of this mixture to cover apples. **5.** Top with ⅓ crumb mixture and rest of apples. Then top with sugar mixture and crumbs for the final layer. **6.** Cover and bake ½ hour. Remove cover and cook another 30 minutes or until apples are tender.

Apple Pie

"There is nothing more wonderful than an apple pie in the oven. The scent of apples and cinnamon fills the air and warms the hearts of everyone in the house. When made well, there are few desserts that are as luscious and versatile as this traditional American favorite. Serve with chocolate, vanilla, or coffee ice cream, with whipped cream (in various flavors) dolloped on top or as suggested below in the variation, cheddar cheese, and a cup of hot chocolate or mulled cider. You can bet guests will ask for seconds." Linda

Ingredients

6 medium (6 cups) tart cooking apples, peeled, sliced ¼"
¾ cup sugar (half white and half brown sugar)
¼ cup all-purpose flour
1 tsp. ground cinnamon
½ tsp. ground nutmeg
4 T. butter, melted

Directions

1. Heat oven to 350°. 2. Combine all filling ingredients *except* apples and butter. 3. Add apples and toss lightly to coat. 4. Spoon mixture into prepared crust (recipe in Index). 5. Pour melted butter over the apple mixture. 6. Place second crust over the apple filling; seal and crimp or flute crust and cut 5 or 6 large slits. 7. Brush crust with the rest of the butter and sprinkle with white sugar. 8. Cover edge of crust with a 2" strip of aluminum foil so it won't get too brown. 9. Bake 35 minutes; remove the foil and bake 10–20 minutes more or until crust is lightly browned and juice begins to bubble through slits in crust. 10. Cool pies for 30 minutes and serve warm.

Variation

If desired, remove pie from oven when lightly browned and bubbly. Run knife through slits in crust. Pour in ½ cup whipping cream evenly through all slits. Return to oven 5 minutes to warm whipping cream.

Baked Alaska

"When I was six, Dad's 12-year-old nephew, David, came to summer with us. He occasionally drove my brother and me crazy with his worldly experience. This friction came to a head when Mom announced she was planning to bake ice cream for Sunday dessert. That was impossible, David gravely warned us.

"My brother, age 4, was an unusually mellow chap who seldom spoke. Provoked by our doubting cousin, however, he rose to Mom's defense insisting she could do anything she said she could do. And when we trooped into the kitchen to witness her magic, she definitely upheld the family honor. Not only did she preserve the frozen treat with a firewall of meringue, but we had to agree it was the best tasting dessert we could ever remember." Lael

Ingredients

1 brick of ice cream, frozen solid
1 sponge or layer cake that is 1" bigger than the ice cream brick on all sides
5 egg whites
$2/3$ cup sugar
$1/2$ tsp. cream of tartar
Granulated sugar for sprinkling

Directions

1. Heat oven to 450°. **2.** For meringue, beat egg whites until very stiff peaks. **3.** Gently stir in sugar and cream of tartar. **4.** Place cake on an unvarnished wooden cutting board that is at least 1" thick and 2" wider than the cake. **5.** Center frozen brick on cake. **6.** Spread meringue over the entire ice cream block and down the sides of the cake, carefully shielding the ice cream with an inch-thick wall of this sweet insulation, sealing it carefully around the edges of the cake. **7.** Sprinkle the top with granulated sugar. **8.** Bake until golden brown in very hot oven until golden brown (about 5 minutes). **9.** Serve immediately.

Bread Pudding

"I always shuddered at the thought of cooking this classic, hoping I would never be that broke. Then friends convinced me to try it at DiMillos floating restaurant in Portland, Maine, and I realized what I'd been missing in my snobbery. Of course, DiMillos served it with a boozy 'secret sauce' from which the alcohol had definitely NOT been cooked off. But I now recommend bread pudding, with or without an alcoholic kick. It's just a brilliant way to save money and stay happy." Lael

Ingredients

1 loaf of stale French bread (white bread is best option) or 1 loaf of raisin bread.
6 eggs
4½ cups milk or light cream

2 cups sugar (white or brown or a 1 cup each combination)
½ cup butter, melted
2 tsp. cinnamon

Additions: ½ tsp. nutmeg, ½ tsp. vanilla, and raisins, or thinly sliced apples, or crushed pineapple. Serve with a hard sauce, vanilla cream sauce or drizzled icing (all recipes in sauce section).

Directions

1. Preheat oven at 350°. **2.** Tear bread into inch-sized pieces and put into nonstick baking dish or one that has been buttered or sprayed with cooking oil. **3.** Mix the other ingredients and pour over the bread. Mix thoroughly. **4.** Cover and bake for 30–40 minutes.

Variation (same directions but for six slices of bread)

4 T. butter, melted
2 cups milk or light cream
¾ cup sugar
4 eggs

1 tsp. cinnamon
1 tsp. vanilla

Brownies

"This recipe was my first real cooking triumph. My family was still living in a remote rural area where, if I wanted sweets, I had to coerce my mother into cooking them. Of course the first thing I learned to make on my own was chocolate fudge, but brownies had so much more class and style, I attempted them shortly after I passed 'Fudge 101.' The results tasted wonderful to me, but I wasn't sure I was just sugar-starved until my usually silent little brother pronounced them "Berry good." Lael

Ingredients

½ cup unsweetened cocoa
½ cup flour
1 cup sugar

2 large eggs, beaten
½ cup butter, melted
1 tsp. vanilla

Additions: ⅔ cup chocolate chips and ⅔ cup slivered almonds or walnuts

Directions

1. Heat oven to 350°. **2.** Combine dry ingredients in a large mixing bowl. **3.** Add eggs, melted butter, vanilla, nuts, and chocolate chips to dry ingredients and mix until thoroughly blended. **4.** Pour into greased pan and bake for 30–40 minutes. Test by inserting a toothpick. If it comes out clean, the brownies are done.

Carrot Cake

"This is, without a doubt, the best carrot cake I've ever tasted and the recipe comes from my sister Diana." Linda

Ingredients
- 2 cups sugar
- 2 cups self-rising flour or regular flour with 1 tsp. baking soda
- 1½ cups Wesson oil
- 4 cups carrots, grated
- 4 eggs
- 4 T. cinnamon

Directions
1. Combine eggs, oil, and carrots. **2.** Add remaining ingredients and mix thoroughly. **3.** Pour into a greased and floured Bundt pan. **4.** Bake in 350° oven for 45 minutes. **5.** Cool completely before turning out. **6.** Frost with butter cream with walnut frosting (recipe in Index).

Chocolate Pecan Squares

"This 'off the wall' recipe may sound bizarre to traditional brownie makers, but give it a try. You'll be pleasantly surprised." Lael

Ingredients
- ¼ lb. butter
- 1 cup graham cracker crumbs
- 1 small pkg. of semisweet chocolate bits
- 1 cup coconut
- 1 cup chopped pecans
- 12 oz. can sweetened condensed milk

Directions
1. Preheat oven to 350°. **2.** Melt butter in 8½ x 11" baking pan. Mix in graham cracker crumbs. **3.** Sprinkle chocolate on top, then coconut, then pecans. **4.** Pour in milk and bake for 30 minutes. **5.** Cool and cut into 1" squares.

Cheese Cake

"I first saw this classic recipe in 1956 when it was the 'next new thing.' A cake out of cheese, we scoffed. But just one taste and everyone in my family was sold. In those dark days in our remote locale, the only way to get this treat was to cook it. This little recipe has seen a lot of mileage but sixty years later it remains my favorite." Lael

Ingredients

16 oz. cottage or ricotta cheese
16 oz. cream cheese
1 cup sugar
6 eggs, separated
2 T. cornstarch
1 tsp. vanilla

Additions: Graham cracker crust or zwieback cookie crust made in a springform pan, 30 well-drained maraschino cherries, cut in half, or ⅓ cup currant or grape jelly, or sliced strawberries to be used for topping.

Directions

1. Preheat oven to 450°. **2.** Put cream cheese and cottage cheese in blender and blend briefly. Then add sugar, beaten egg yolks, cornstarch, and vanilla, and blend just enough to mix. **3.** Beat egg whites stiff but not dry, and fold into cheese mixture. Pour into ungreased springform pan with crust already placed inside. **4.** Bake for 5 minutes. Lower oven heat to 350° and bake one hour longer. Chill before serving.

Cherry or Strawberry Rhubarb Pie

"Rhubarb is a very tart vegetable that is typically coupled with sweet fruits in preserves, sauces, and desserts. Thought to cut the risk of cancer and to have anti-oxidant, anti-inflammatory, and anti-allergy properties, rhubarb comes in many varieties and is versatile. However, eat the stalks only, as the leaves contain oxalic acid and can be toxic. My daughter introduced me to rhubarb with this pie, and I am a fan now." Linda

Ingredients
1 cup sugar
4 cups chopped rhubarb or scissor-cut into small pieces
1 can cherry pie filling
¼ cup minute tapioca
2 uncooked piecrusts

Directions
1. Preheat oven to 425°. **2.** On lightly floured surface, roll out half the pastry; fit into a deep pie dish. **3.** In a bowl, stir sugar with tapioca; add cherry filling and rhubarb, tossing to coat. Pour over piecrust. **4.** Roll out remaining pastry and fit over top; trim and flute edge. Brush egg over pastry and sprinkle with sugar. Cut vents; place on baking sheet. **5.** Bake for 15 minutes. Reduce heat to 375°; bake for 35 to 45 minutes or until golden and bubbly.

Variation
Substitute the cherry filling with 4 cups of strawberries.

Chocolate Fondue

"For years, my family brought in the New Year with a fondue dinner. We dipped crusty French bread into Swiss cheese melted with wine and nutmeg, sizzled slivers of sirloin in hot oil, and cooked little red potatoes in a garlic/dill butter sauce, but the crowning glory was the chocolate fondue in which we dipped pieces of angel food cake, bananas, strawberries, mandarin oranges and miniature cream puffs." Linda

Ingredients

12 oz. milk chocolate
¾ cup light cream

1 to 2 T. cherry brandy, Kahlua, orange-flavored liqueur, or 2 tsp. powdered instant coffee or ½ tsp. mint extract

Directions

1. Melt chocolate in cream over low heat, stirring until smooth.
2. Add desired flavoring right before serving.

Variation

White fondue—substitute white almond bark for the milk chocolate and decrease light cream to ⅓ cup.

Chocolate Mousse Cake

"No holiday is complete for my son, Derek, if I don't serve this cake. It is luscious, impressive, and so very easy to make. The best part is that I must make it the day before my gathering, leaving me one less dish to make the day of. You will not have any leftovers; it is just that good.

"This recipe came to me from my Aunt Grace who gave out the recipe to few people. When asked, she would say that she would be glad to bring the cake. She gave it to me because I lived out of town and there was little danger that I would show up with the cake to family events. I entered her recipe into a contest, and it won first prize." Linda

Ingredients

3 pkg. ladyfingers
1 large pkg. semisweet morsels
½ pint whipping cream
6 eggs, separated
5 T. water
½ tsp. vanilla

Directions

1. Melt chocolate chips in a mixing bowl with water and vanilla (can be melted in a microwave). **2.** Add egg yolks to melted chocolate and mix on high for five minutes. **3.** Beat egg whites until stiff and fold gently into chocolate mixture. **4.** Beat whipping cream and fold gently into chocolate mixture. **5.** Line springform pan (or large serving bowl) with ladyfingers, around the edge and across the bottom. **6.** Pour in half the chocolate mixture and put on another layer of ladyfingers. **7.** Pour on remainder of chocolate mixture. Cover and refrigerate overnight. **8.** Before serving, decorate with whipped cream (from the can is great).

Note: Though this can be made in a big glass bowl, it is best in a springform pan as it holds the ladyfingers and mousse together as it solidifies. When the outside of the pan is released the next day, the cake can stand alone and looks lovely when sliced. It can also be taken to the table on the bottom of the springform pan.

Creamy Pies

"We had a mulberry and an apple tree in our back yard in Maryland and little had to be done to them (no fertilizer or pesticides) to produce delicious fruit. My grandmother also had numerous fruit trees in her yard including a cherry tree that we kids loved climbing and eating from until we were almost sick. I was always so impressed when my grandmother would come outside to gather the fruit because I knew that in minutes and with great ease, she would have whipped out a couple of hot, oozing fruit pies that melted in our mouths." Linda

Ingredients for two pies

2 eggs, separated
2/3 cup sugar
3 T. flour, heaping
1 1/2 cups milk
2 1/2 T. butter
2 piecrusts

Directions

1. In mixer, slightly beat yolks. Add sugar and flour; add milk and stir until smooth. **2.** Pour into heavy saucepan and stir over medium heat. When mixture begins to thicken and bubble, cook about one minute more. Be careful not to scorch. **3.** Remove from heat and add butter. **4.** Pour into a baked or crumb piecrust.

Variations

Almond Pie: After fully cooked, add 1/4 cup slivered almonds and 1 tsp. almond extract. Top with meringue and sprinkle with a few almonds.

Banana Pie: Pour filling over sliced bananas in a vanilla wafer crust. Meringue can be added.

Chocolate Pie: Add 2 T. cocoa to flour before cooking. Add 1 tsp. vanilla after fully cooked.

Coconut Pie: After fully cooked, add 1/2 cup shredded coconut and 1 tsp. lemon juice; sprinkle a little coconut on top of meringue.

Lemon Pie: After fully cooked, add 4 T. fresh lemon juice and 1/4 tsp. grated lemon rind (no vanilla). Top with meringue.

Meringue

"Many dishes call for stiffly beaten egg whites or the sweetened version which is called meringue. This sure-fire version works wonderfully for topping pies." Linda

Ingredients

2 egg whites (for higher topping, increase this recipe. Meringue shrinks both in the oven and in the refrigerator)

4 T. sugar
½ tsp. vanilla
½ tsp. almond flavoring
⅛ tsp. cream of tartar per egg white

Directions

1. Beat egg whites until frothy. **2.** Add cream of tartar and beat more. **3.** After egg whites are thickened and stiff, add sugar and flavorings. **4.** If used to top a pie, seal edges and bake 10 minutes in 350° oven.

Note: Some recipes call for beaten egg whites to be stirred or "folded" into a mixture of other ingredients. This should be done very slowly and carefully. Instead of stirring round and round in the bowl, you literally fold the beaten whites into the mixture by carefully pulling the mixture over the whites with your spoon. This process keeps air in the mixture and ensures greater height and lightness.

Piecrust (Baked)

Ingredients
½ cup butter, room temperature
⅓ cup sugar
¼ tsp. vanilla
1 cup flour

Directions
1. Preheat oven to 450°. **2.** In a small bowl, cream together butter, sugar, and vanilla. **3.** Blend in the flour. **4.** Pat dough into the bottom and up the sides to the rim of an ungreased 9" pie pan. If you're using a second crust to top the pie, wet the end of the lower crust along the rim slightly with water or milk. **5.** Whether you top pie with a second crust or simply add a filling to bake "topless," you will want to crinkle the edge of piecrust around the rim of the dish in a decorative fashion. You can press top and bottom crusts together along the pie plate rim with the tines of a fork or pinch them together by pushing them with the thumb of one hand into the "V" made by the thumb and index finger of your other hand. If you are using just one crust, pinch it along the rim to make it stand up prettily.

Piecrust (Unbaked)

Ingredients
2 cups graham crackers or chocolate wafer crumbs, crushed
⅓ cup sugar
⅓ cup melted butter
1 tsp. cinnamon (optional)

Directions
1. Combine all ingredients and mix well. **2.** Press firmly into a pie plate and chill.

Cream Puffs

"My Aunt Inez, who was first lady at the huge dairy farm established three generations ago by our Abbott clan in Vermont, thought nothing of cooking meals for ten or twelve people, because dinners usually included hired help as well as family. She was an excellent cook, but few of us ever recovered from the practical joke she cooked up one April Fools' Day. Cream Puffs, her specialty, were on the menu and everyone raced through the entrée to enjoy them. Problem was, she had filled them with a batch of laundry soap she had whipped up to look exactly like whipped cream." *Lael*

"Now, there's a story I want to know the end of!" *Linda*

Ingredients

½ cup flour
½ cup milk or water
¼ cup butter, plus enough to grease baking tin
⅛ tsp. salt
2 eggs
3 cups whipped cream or custard

Directions

1. Preheat oven to 350°. **2.** Heat milk or water, add butter, and bring to a boil. **3.** Add flour and salt, stirring batter until it leaves the sides of the pan and forms a ball. **4.** Remove from heat and add eggs, one at a time, beating the first until well blended before blending in the second. **5.** Place batter in 2" round mounds on greased tin, at least 2" apart. **6.** Bake 30 minutes before reducing heat to 300° and baking an additional 5 minutes. (Test for doneness by removing one puff from oven. If it doesn't fall, it is cooked through). **7.** Remove puffs from oven and cool. Cut a slit in the side of each and fill with whipped cream or custard. Then serve immediately or be very sure they are stored in a cool place, because filled shells can spoil quickly without showing any signs of trouble.

Flan

"Flan is a traditional Mexican dessert and there are many versions. This recipe is prized for its simplicity." Linda

Ingredients (for ramekin presentation)

1½ cups sugar
6 large eggs
2, 13 oz. cans evaporated milk
1, 14 oz. can sweetened condensed milk
1 tsp. vanilla

Directions

1. Preheat oven to 325°. Use 6 ramekins (a small dish for baking and serving in) and a large baking pan to put them in.
2. Pour 1 cup sugar in warm pan over medium heat. Constantly stir sugar until it browns and becomes caramel. Quickly pour 2–3 tablespoons of caramel in each ramekin, tilting it to swirl the caramel around the sides. Reheat caramel if it starts to harden.
3. In a mixer or with a whisk, blend the eggs together. Mix in the milks and then slowly mix in the ½ cup sugar, then the vanilla. Blend smooth after each ingredient is added.
4. Pour custard into caramel-lined ramekins. Place ramekins in a large glass or ceramic baking dish and fill dish with 1–2" of hot water.
5. Bake for 45 minutes in the water-bath and check with a knife just to the side of the center. If knife comes out clean, it's ready.
6. Remove and let cool. Let each ramekin cool in refrigerator for 1 hour. Invert each ramekin onto a small plate; the caramel sauce will flow over the custard.

Traditional Chocolate Fudge

"Because we were raised cash-challenged in an isolated rural area with little chance to shop, sweets were a rare treat for my little brother and me. Sometimes, though, on cold, rainy days when we couldn't go out to play and our mother grew tired of our squabbling, she would experiment with a candy recipe while we watched her every move in rapt attention.

"Molasses taffy was the most fun because we got to smear our hands with butter and 'pull' a cooked batch until it cooled, turned pale, and could be dried to sweet excellence on greased waxed paper. However, fudge was our all-time favorite, and it was simple enough so that we soon learned to make it ourselves.

"Surprisingly, I lost my sweet tooth as an adult but I'd give a lot to return to another session of fudge making around our dependable wood stove in rural Maine. We'd never heard of pecans or butterscotch chips in those days, but Linda's updated version is a welcome addition to our treasury." Lael

Ingredients

2 cups white sugar
½ cup cocoa
1 cup milk
4 T. butter
1 tsp. vanilla extract

Directions

1. Grease an 8 x 8" square baking pan. Set aside. **2.** Combine sugar, cocoa, and milk in a medium saucepan. Stir to blend. Bring to a boil, stirring constantly. Reduce heat and simmer. Do not stir again. **3.** Place candy thermometer in pan and cook until temperature reaches 238° F (114° C). If you're not using a thermometer, then cook until a drop of this mixture forms a soft ball in a cup of cold water. Feel the ball with your fingers to make sure it is the right consistency. It should flatten when pressed between your fingers. **4.** Remove from heat. Add butter or margarine and vanilla extract. Beat with a wooden spoon until the fudge loses its sheen. Do not under beat. **5.** Pour into prepared pan and let cool. Cut into about sixty squares.

Butterscotch Fudge

"There is nothing as rich and decadent as Chocolate Fudge, however, if you want to change up perfection with a little jazz, try flavoring it with Butterscotch. Making fudge with chocolate and butterscotch chips is a lot easier, too." Linda

Ingredients
1 cup chocolate chips
1 cup butterscotch chips
1, 14 oz. can sweetened condensed milk
1 tsp. pure vanilla extract
1 cup pecans (any type of nut will work)

Directions
1. Melt chocolate chips, butterscotch chips, and condensed milk in double boiler on medium heat. **2.** When smooth, remove from heat. Add vanilla and nuts. **3.** Scoop into a 9 x 9" baking dish and chill until set for approximately 10 minutes.

Pecan Pie

"This is another favorite of my daughter, Tricia, because I load the pie with more pecans than most do and the filling is stick-to-your-teeth thick rather than gel-like." Linda

Ingredients
3 large eggs
½ cup sugar
4 T. butter, melted
1 tsp. vanilla
2 cups pecans
1 cup dark corn syrup

Directions
1. Follow directions for baking and cooling 1 pie shell. Then reset oven to 350°. **2.** Beat eggs. Add sugar and beat again. **3.** Mix in butter and vanilla. **4.** Pour in corn syrup and mix. **5.** Fold in pecans. **6.** Bake for 1 hour.

Variation
Add 1 cup semisweet chocolate chips.

Golden Fruitcake

"All of you who think you hate fruitcake need to try this recipe, especially at the holidays. It will make fruitcake converts of all who take even one morsel. A Bundt (molded) pan turns out pretty cake. If you can afford to add one to your cooking arsenal, they can be cheap and easy to find, even in a dollar store." Linda

Ingredients

1 pkg. yellow cake mix
1 large pkg. of instant vanilla pudding
4 eggs
½ cup oil
1 cup milk
Sweet glaze (recipe in Index)

Additions: 2 cups golden raisins, 1 cup chopped apricots (and/or mango), and 1½ cup chopped walnuts, 1 tsp. vanilla, and 1 tsp. brandy extract.

Directions

1. Preheat oven to 350°. **2.** Mix all ingredients together thoroughly and pour into a greased and floured pan. **3.** Bake for 40 minutes. Cool completely before turning out and glazing.

Key Lime Pie

"This is a favorite dessert with my New England peer group, even though most of us never even knew limes existed while we were growing up, which is why you have Linda's formula here instead of mine. Yankees should not have the audacity to craft this dessert without special dispensation from someone who realized early there was more citrus in life than oranges and lemons." Lael

Ingredients

- 9" graham cracker pie crust
- 2, 14-ounce cans sweetened condensed milk
- ½ cup key lime juice, fresh or bottled
- 6 egg yolks (egg whites can be used for a meringue)

Directions

1. Blend milk and egg yolks at slow speed until smooth. 2. Add key lime juice and finish blending. 3. Pour into piecrust. 4. Bake in preheated 300° oven for 15 minutes. 5. Cool pie 20 minutes before refrigerating. 6. Serve chilled key lime pie with whipped cream topping or baked meringue.

Variation

Ingredients

- 1, 14 oz. can sweetened condensed milk
- ¾ egg substitute
- ½ cup fresh lime juice
- 2 tsp. lime zest
- 1, 8 oz. container frozen whipped topping, thawed or whipped cream
- 1, 6 oz. graham cracker crust

Directions

1. Preheat oven to 350°. 2. Whisk together first 4 ingredients until well blended. 3. Pour mixture into piecrust; place pie on baking sheet. 4. Bake for 17 minutes or until pie is set. Remove pie from baking sheet to wire rack and let cool completely for one hour. Chill overnight. Top with whipped cream.

Lemon Bars

"California friends bought a tiny lemon tree which I watched grow into a prolific producer in just a few years. What to do with a zillion beautiful lemons? Here is our favorite answer." Lael

Ingredients

1 cup butter, softened
2 cups sugar (½ cup to cream with butter for crust and 1½ cups to add to flour for topping)
2¼ cups flour (2 cups for crust and ¼ cup for topping)
4 eggs
2 juiced lemons

Directions

1. Preheat oven to 350°. **2.** In a medium bowl, cream together softened butter and ½ cup sugar, then mix in 2 cups flour. **3.** Press into the bottom of an ungreased 9 x 13" pan. **4.** Bake for 15 to 20 minutes in the preheated oven or until firm and golden. **5.** In another bowl, whisk together the remaining 1½ cups sugar and ¼ cup flour. **6.** Whisk in the eggs and lemon juice. Pour over the baked crust. **7.** Bake for an additional 20 minutes. The bars will firm up as they cool. **8.** Cut into uniform 2" squares and arrange in a checkerboard fashion.

Mud Pie

"I've seen the origins of Mud Pie attributed to every state along the Mississippi, but I never cared who thought up this concoction. I don't much care for pies and had it depended on me, the only ones in this collection would be apple and pecan. Knowing Linda and her family prefer dessert, I left that part of our cookbook to her, but I was shocked when she included Mud Pie on her list. You see, I love Mud Pie so much that it seldom occurs to me that it **is** a pie. Instead, I've always viewed it as a little slice of something that just fell from heaven." *Lael*

Ingredients

1 pkg. chocolate wafers (can be kept in the freezer)
¼ cup butter, melted
1 gallon coffee ice cream, softened
1½ cups hot fudge sauce
½ cup walnuts
Whipped cream

Directions

1. Crush wafers (either in a food processor or in a plastic bag with a rolling pin). **2.** Add butter and mix well. Press into a 9" pie shell and freeze for 10 minutes. **3.** Mound ice cream in pie shell and freeze. **4.** Cover with cold fudge sauce and nuts, and freeze for 10 hours. **5.** Add whipped cream before serving.

Pumpkin Soufflé

"My favorite part of fall, besides gorgeous color and cooler weather, is the pumpkin. Such a versatile vegetable, it is the main ingredient of many delicious soups and casseroles. But its true claim to fame is the part it plays in desserts. When my children were young, we always carved at least one mammoth pumpkin in October, stripped it of the pulp to steam for pie filling to bake then and freeze for Thanksgiving and Christmas, and roasted the seeds for a nutritious snack. Fresh pumpkin over canned makes pies and soufflés lighter in flavor and color but canned is certainly fine and allows pumpkin treats all year round." Linda

Ingredients

32 oz. pureed pumpkin, canned or fresh
1 cup white sugar
1 cup brown sugar
6 eggs, slightly beaten
3 cups evaporated milk
5 T. cinnamon
1 T. nutmeg

Additions: 1 tsp. salt, 2 tsp. cloves, 2 tsp. ginger, 1 tsp. vanilla, whipped cream

Directions

1. Beat eggs slightly. Add sugar and mix thoroughly. **2.** Then add spices and milk, and mix again. **3.** Pour into ovenproof custard dishes or ramekins. **4.** Bake for 40 minutes at 350° or until golden brown on top. Top with whipped cream.

Variations

1. Perfect Pumpkin Pie—pour the above filling into two or three pie shells and bake for 45 minutes in a 350° oven.
2. Pumpkin Crunch Cake—mix together thoroughly and pour into a greased, 9 x 13" pan a 15 oz. can of pumpkin, 3 eggs, one 12 oz. can of evaporated milk, 1½ cups sugar, and ½ tsp. salt. Sprinkle a box of yellow cake mix evenly over the top of the mixture. Top with 1½ cups of chopped pecans. Drizzle 1 cup melted butter over pecans and bake for 55 minutes in 350° oven.

Rice Pudding

"Never fear if you have cooked too much rice. Turn it into a delicious pudding that will have your guests asking for seconds." Linda

Ingredients

2 cups cooked rice
1 ⅓ cups milk
3 ½ T. sugar

1 T. butter plus additional to grease baking dish
2 eggs
1 tsp. vanilla

Additions: 1 cup raisins or chopped dates

Directions

1. Preheat oven to 325° and grease baking dish. **2.** Combine all ingredients, stirring lightly with a fork. **3.** Pour in pudding and bake until pudding is firm (about ½ hour).

Turtle Cake

"This cake is wonderful—a dessert that will truly wow your guests." Linda

Ingredients

1 box of German chocolate cake mix
16 oz. can of evaporated milk
18 oz. jar of caramel sauce

2 cups whipped topping or fresh whipped cream
½ cup chopped pecans
Toffee chips

Directions

1. Follow directions on box to make batter; pour into a greased and floured 9 x 13" pan. **2.** Sprinkle chopped pecans evenly over the top of batter; then bake. **3.** When the cake is done, use the handle of a wooden spoon to poke holes in the still hot cake. **4.** Pour evaporated milk evenly all over cake. **5.** Pour caramel evenly all over cake and refrigerate for two hours. **6.** Cover the top of the cake with Cool Whip or whipped cream. **7.** Sprinkle with toffee chips.

Strawberry Bavarian Cream

Bavarian cream is a 17th century recipe that apparently came from German royalty who could afford to hire French chefs. It remains a culinary delight." *Lael*

Ingredients
10 oz. pkg. sweetened frozen strawberries, thawed
1 pkg. strawberry flavored gelatin (to serve 4)
1 cup boiling water
2½ cups whipping cream, chilled
2½ T. confectioners' sugar
¾ tsp. vanilla

Directions
1. Drain strawberries, reserving juice. **2.** Combine gelatin and boiling water in small bowl. Stir until gelatin is dissolved. Add enough water to strawberry juice to measure 1 cup and stir into gelatin. Refrigerate until gelatin is slightly thickened. Beat gelatin until foamy. **3.** Beat 1 cup whipping cream with sugar and vanilla until stiff peaks form in large bowl. Fold into gelatin with strawberry mixture. Chill and scoop into dessert dishes. Garnish with more whipped cream and a strawberry.

Strawberries Devonshire

"Until the day I discovered Strawberries Devonshire, I always figured elegant desserts would have to be complicated. Not so with this simple classic which is inexpensive in season, takes little time to prepare, and is impossible to mess up. It's a no-brainer if your guests are rich and famous and you wish to appear more sophisticated than you may be." *Lael*

"When I tasted this the first time, I was hooked, but I wanted to simplify it even further and have it available even if I did not have whipping cream on hand, so I added brown sugar and vanilla to the sour cream, and it is still wonderful not only with strawberries but also with bananas." *Linda*

Ingredients
4 cups fresh strawberries, hulled and rinsed
½ cup sour cream
¼ cup brown sugar
1 ½ cups whipped cream
1 tsp. vanilla extract

Additions: 1 tsp. rum extract, 1 T. Grand Marnier, ¼ cup orange juice, or ⅛ cup lemon juice.

Directions
1. Whip cream and add desired flavor. **2.** Layer sour cream, brown sugar, and half-whipped cream mixture in four dessert dishes. **3.** Divide strawberries between dessert dishes. **4.** Put the leftover whipped cream mixture on top.

Torte

"One of the most delicious tortes I have ever had was in Vienna, Austria, at the Sacher Hotel, which, by the way, became famous because of its torte. Since 1832, its recipe has been kept secret. The dessert is a chocolate cake, thinly coated by hand with a special apricot jam and covered in a chocolate icing that is to die for. Now, ours is a bit different, but I think just as decadent." Linda

Ingredients

- 1 pkg. fudge brownie mix (1 lb. 3.8 ounces)
- 1 pkg. chocolate or white chocolate pudding and pie filling mix (4 serving size)
- 1/3 cup miniature semisweet chocolate chips
- 1 1/4 cups milk
- 1, 8 oz. container frozen whip cream topping, thawed or fresh whipped cream (3 1/2 cups)
- 1 pt. (2 cups) raspberries or strawberries

Directions

1. Heat oven to 325°. Spray bottom only of a springform pan with cooking spray. Make brownie mix as directed on pkg. using water, oil, and eggs. Spread in pan. Bake 45–50 minutes or until toothpick comes out clean. **2.** Cool completely (do not remove side of pan). **3.** Cook pudding and fold in whipped cream and chocolate chips. Pour over brownies. **4.** Cover and freeze at least 4 hours before serving. Remove side of pan. **5.** Serve with berries. Store covered in freezer.

Trifle

"A proper English trifle is made with real egg custard poured over sponge cake soaked in fruit and sherry and topped with whipped cream. It originated as a way to use up cake that had gone stale (Who knew there were people who let that happen!). Americans have varied the traditional strawberry, sponge cake confection a bit. They use angel food cake, pound cake, or bake a white or yellow cake, and they use pudding flavors like chocolate, banana, or butterscotch.

"Sometimes fresh or frozen fruits like peach and raspberry are used rather than jellies, and sometimes fruits are combined, but whatever the choices, the dessert is served in a large-stemmed, clear glass trifle bowl so the colors and layers can be appreciated." Linda

Ingredients

1 angel food cake
15 oz. pkg. frozen strawberry halves, thawed
¼ cup sugar
1 pkg. vanilla pudding (to serve 4), not instant pudding
1 cup chilled whipping cream
¼ cup toasted slivered almonds

Directions

1. Cook pudding according to directions and cool. **2.** Arrange half the pieces of cake in a two-quart glass serving bowl. Pour half the strawberries with juice over cake; spread with 1 cup of pudding. Repeat with remaining cake pieces, strawberries, and pudding. Cover and chill at least 4 hours. **3.** In chilled bowl, beat cream and sugar until stiff; spread over trifle. **4.** Sprinkle with almonds and garnish with strawberries. **5.** Spoon into dessert dishes.

Variations

Banana Trifle—substitute white or yellow cake mix for angel food cake and 2 large bananas, sliced, for the strawberries, or Chocolate Trifle—substitute devil's food cake, chocolate pudding and either strawberries or raspberries, or Black Forest Trifle—devil's food cake mix, chocolate pudding and 1 can of cherry pie filling.

Yummy Sheet Cakes

"The recipe below is extremely versatile. You can use any combination of cake mixes and puddings, so try a yellow cake mix with lemon pudding, butterscotch, or cheesecake pudding, or a devil's food cake mix with chocolate or egg custard pudding, or a white cake mix with vanilla, banana cream, or coconut pudding. Any combo works, so get creative." Linda

Ingredients
1 cake mix
1 box of pudding
5 eggs
2 cups sour cream
½ cup melted butter
1, 12 oz. pkg. of semisweet chocolate chips

Directions
1. Preheat oven to 350°. **2.** Grease and flour 9 x 13" pan. **3.** Mix first five ingredients thoroughly. **4.** Add chocolate chips and mix. **5.** Pour into pan and bake for 45 minutes or until a toothpick comes out clean.

Vanilla Custard

"You'll find plenty of prepackaged custard mixes, but none of them I've ever tried beat this simple recipe for flavor and charm." Lael

Ingredients
2 cups milk
3 T. sugar
6 eggs
½ tsp. vanilla

Directions
1. Heat milk and add sugar. Cook and stir until just dissolved. Do not boil. **2.** Beat eggs and pour heated milk over eggs while stirring constantly. **3.** Place in double boiler and cook over hot water. Do not let milk boil. **4.** Cook until sauce thickens to coat the spoon. **5.** Add vanilla and chill (unless serving immediately). **6.** Serve in individual dishes, in cream puffs, or over crepes, fresh berries and fruit pies.

Variation

Ingredients
4 cups milk
⅔ cup sugar
6 eggs
1 T. vanilla
½ tsp. salt
½ cup brown sugar

Directions
1. Beat eggs and add sugar, salt, and vanilla. **2.** Add milk, mix again, and cook until thickened. **3.** Spread brown sugar on the bottom of a large glass bowl or the bottom of individual ramekins. **4.** Pour hot custard on top of brown sugar and refrigerate overnight before serving.

Dessert Sauces

"You might feel like sauces seem redundant on an already sweet dessert, but just like on entrees, a dessert sauce heightens flavor and elevates presentation. Using sauces on your offerings will wow your guests and make you feel like a real chef." Linda

Chocolate Syrup

"Good for shakes, smoothies, ice-cream sodas, and the like. Great added to coffee to make a mocha drink." Linda

Ingredients
- ½ cup unsweetened cocoa powder
- ½ tsp. ground cinnamon
- 2½ cups sugar
- 2 cups water

Directions
1. Combine cocoa with cinnamon and water and bring to a boil. Stir in sugar slowly over medium heat. **2.** As soon as sugar is dissolved, remove from heat and cool. It can be stored in a glass jar in refrigerator for up to two weeks.

Praline Sauce

"Serve this sauce over French toast, waffles or pancakes for a particularly special treat." Linda

Ingredients
- ¾ cup butter
- ¾ cup brown sugar
- ¾ cup maple syrup
- ½ tsp. vanilla
- 1 cup toasted pecans

Directions
1. In a saucepan, melt butter and mix in brown sugar. **2.** Add in maple syrup and warm thoroughly. **3.** Add pecans.

Fruit Sauce

"Serve as a dip for berries and bananas." Linda

Ingredients

1 cup whipping cream
1 cup sour cream
1 cup brown sugar

1 tsp. vanilla
¼ cup rum or 1 T. rum
   extract (optional)

Directions

1. Beat whipping cream until stiff. **2.** Mix well sour cream, brown sugar, vanilla, and rum. **3.** Fold into whipped cream.

Variations

Pour vanilla yogurt combined with cinnamon on thinly sliced green apples.

Ingredients

4 oz. cream cheese, softened
2, 8 oz. containers
  vanilla yogurt

½ tsp. cinnamon
½ cup brown sugar

Directions

1. Use an electric mixer or blender to combine all the ingredients.
2. Chill and use on fresh fruit.

Hard Sauce

"This recipe is so simple and so good that it's hard to imagine not using it on cold or hot desserts like apple pie or steamed pudding. Not only is the flavor perfect, but the cold sauce melting on a hot dish will delight other senses. It was a staple of my New England childhood." Lael

Ingredients
⅓ cup butter, softened
1 cup confectioner's sugar
1 tsp. vanilla or other flavorings like brandy or rum

Directions
1. Cream butter in a medium-sized mixing bowl with a big spoon until soft. Mash in sugar a little at a time and add flavoring.
2. Refrigerate until needed. This recipe stores well in a glass jar.

Variation
Use granulated sugar instead of confectioner's sugar. It adds an interesting crunch.

Lemon Cream Sauce

"I find this formula a very clever invention. Try it with cake or bread pudding to produce a winning dessert." Lael

Ingredients
⅓ cup whipping (heavy) cream
1 pkg. cream cheese (4 oz.), softened
¼ cup sugar
2 tsp. grated lemon peel

Directions
1. Beat whipping cream in a mixer until stiff; set aside. **2.** Then beat cream cheese on high speed until fluffy. **3.** Stir in sugar and lemon peel. Gently fold in whipped cream.

Hot Chocolate Sauce

"If you have only an occasional sweet tooth and buy a jar of chocolate sauce at the store, chances are it will spoil before you can finish it. Here is a recipe that you can cook up from easily stored ingredients for any occasion. And you probably won't have to worry about leftovers, especially if you serve it over vanilla or coffee ice cream." Linda

Ingredients
4 oz. unsweetened chocolate (usually two squares)
1 cup light corn syrup
2 T. butter
½ tsp. vanilla

Directions
1. Melt chocolate in corn syrup in small saucepan over low heat. **2.** Remove from heat and stir in vanilla and butter. Serve immediately.

Vanilla Sauce

"Delicious on pound cake or warm bread pudding, over cobbler or fresh fruits." Linda

Ingredients
2 T. cornstarch
1 cup granulated sugar
1 cup water
1 cup light cream or half-and-half
4 T. butter
2 tsp. vanilla

Directions
1. In a bowl, whisk the cornstarch and sugar together until well blended. Set aside. **2.** In a saucepan, bring the water and cream to a boil. **3.** Whisk in the sugar and cornstarch mixture and simmer, stirring, for about 2 minutes until thickened and bubbly. **4.** Remove from heat and stir in the butter, vanilla, and salt.

Hot Caramel Sauce

"Caramel has always seemed exotic to me. The term goes back to the Latin word for sugar cane (cannamellis), and the chemistry involves heating the sugar to get rid of its water content. It sounds simple enough and this recipe is a good one. However, you have to watch carefully during the cooking process, so you won't overdo it." Lael

Ingredients

1½ cups sugar
½ cup light corn syrup
¼ cup butter, melted

1 cup light cream
1 tsp. vanilla

Directions

1. Mix sugar, corn syrup, 4 T. butter, and ½ cup cream together in saucepan and bring to a boil. **2.** Mix remaining butter and cream together; add to boiled sugar mixture and stir constantly until thickened. **3.** When it is the desired consistency, remove from heat and add vanilla and salt.

Frostings and Icings

"The most obvious difference between frosting, icing and glaze is the texture. Frosting is creamy, opaque in color and is much thicker in density. Because it can hold a shape, it is used for making rosettes and shells on a cake. Icing is generally made with a sugar base and egg whites, so it is thinner in consistency, clearer in color and hardens up much like a shell when it dries. A glaze is made from a simple mixture of confectioner's sugar and water. It is far more like a glossy liquid into which food items like donuts are dipped. Glazes can also be made from fruit or fruit juice and are often dripped onto pastries." Linda

Chocolate Frosting

"Because there are rows of canned frosting on the shelves alongside sugar and flour and cake mixes, we buy a can mindlessly. We have forgotten just how unbelievably easy it is to make our own frosting without any preservatives, food colorings, and other ingredients that are not even recognizable. Think fresh and healthier ingredients." Linda

Ingredients
1 cup granulated sugar
¼ cup cocoa
¼ cup butter
¼ cup milk
1 tsp. vanilla

Directions
1. Mix ingredients together in a saucepan. Bring to a boil for 1 minute. **2.** Add vanilla. Cool partially, then beat with a mixer for 3 minutes or until spreadable.

Cream Cheese Frosting

"This is an invaluable frosting in a pinch and often a first choice without one." Lael

Ingredients
2, 8 oz. pkgs. cream cheese, softened
½ cup butter, softened
2 cups sifted confectioners' sugar
1 tsp. vanilla

Additions: ¼ cup maple syrup, 2 T. rum, 5 T. bourbon, 1 cup chopped pecans

Directions
1. In a medium bowl, cream together the butter and cream cheese until well blended. **2.** Mix in the vanilla. **3.** Then gradually stir in the confectioners' sugar. **4.** Mix in desired additions.

Maple Syrup Frosting

"I'm still hooked on this wonderful recipe, which comes from my family homestead, now the Goodrich Maple Farm, but please don't try it with a phony or watered-down maple syrup. It just will not be the same." Lael

Ingredients
1 cup pure maple syrup
2 unbeaten egg whites
¼ cup chopped nuts

Directions
1. Cook maple syrup in a medium-sized saucepan until ¼ tsp. of it thickens almost to a hard ball when dropped into a glass of cold water. **2.** Place egg whites in a large mixing bowl and beat in thickened syrup a little at a time until mixture stiffens into good frosting consistency even though icing will remain soft. **3.** Frost. **4.** Scatter top of cake with nuts.

Cake and Pastry Glaze

"Add glazing to French toast, bread pudding or cinnamon rolls and you have a delicious breakfast or brunch offering." Linda

Ingredients
1 cup powdered sugar
1 T. milk
1 tsp. vegetable oil

Directions
Mix ingredients and drip over cake or pastry.

Variation (especially good on bread pudding)

Ingredients
1 cup powdered sugar
1 tsp. vanilla
1 tsp. cinnamon
Milk to moisten

Directions
Mix ingredients and drizzle on when cake or pudding is warm.

Chocolate Glaze

Chocolate glaze is perfect for donuts, cookies, and dripping on cake. Linda

Ingredients
¾ cup semisweet chocolate chips
3 T. butter
1 T. light corn syrup
¼ tsp. vanilla

Directions
1. In a double boiler over hot, but not boiling, water, combine chocolate chips, butter, and corn syrup. Stir until chips are melted and mixture is smooth, and then add vanilla. 2. Spread warm glaze over top of cake, letting it drizzle down the sides.

Peanut Butter Frosting

"Before serving this dessert, check for peanut allergies. If your guests have sound constitutions, this unusual delight will garner rave reviews." Lael

Ingredients
½ cup butter
1 cup creamy peanut butter
4 cups confectioners' sugar
⅓ cup cream

Directions
1. In a large bowl, beat butter and peanut butter until light and fluffy. **2.** Slowly beat in ½ of the confectioners' sugar. **3.** Mix in ¼ cup of the cream. **4.** Beat in the remaining confectioners' sugar. If necessary, add a little more cream or milk until the frosting reaches a good spreading consistency.

Vanilla Frosting

"This recipe is unusual in that it has a white sauce base. Try it with real vanilla flavoring, and you'll become an advocate." Lael

Ingredients
1 cup milk
3 T. flour
½ lb. (2 sticks) butter
1 cup granulated sugar
2 tsp. vanilla

Directions
1. In a saucepan, make a white sauce of milk and flour. It will be very thick. Boil for a few minutes. Cool completely. **2.** Cream butter. Add sugar and vanilla. Combine with white sauce and beat on high speed in a food mixer for about 5 minutes.

Butter Cream Frosting

"This delicious frosting can be used for any cake, but it is particularly fabulous with chopped walnuts on the included carrot cake recipe." Linda

Ingredients

8 oz. pkg. cream cheese, softened
½ cup butter, softened
1 lb. confectioners' sugar
1 tsp. vanilla
Pinch of salt
½ cup walnuts

Directions

1. In a bowl, cream butter and cream cheese together. **2.** Add the rest of the ingredients and frost a cooled cake. **3.** Refrigerate so frosting will solidify.

Variation

Ingredients

½ cup unsalted butter, softened
1 ½ tsp. vanilla
2 cups confectioners' sugar, sifted
2 T. milk
Food coloring, if desired

Directions

1. Cream softened butter until smooth and fluffy. **2.** Gradually beat in confectioners' sugar until fully incorporated. Beat in vanilla. **3.** Pour in milk and beat for an additional 3–4 minutes. **4.** Add food coloring, if using, and beat for thirty seconds until smooth or until desired color is reached.

Whipped Cream

"Though those spray cans are convenient, whipping your own cream is a piece of cake, and you can add your own flavors for distinction and variety." Linda

Ingredients
- 1 cup whipping cream, heavy
- 2 T. sugar, white or brown depending on desired flavor
- 1 tsp. cornstarch
- 1 tsp. flavoring (vanilla, mint, amaretto, walnut, or almond)

Directions
Beat all ingredients in chilled medium bowl with electric mixer on high speed until stiff.

Variation (for thickened Whipped Cream)

Ingredients
- 8 oz. pkg. cream cheese, softened
- ½ cup sugar
- 1 tsp. vanilla
- ½ tsp. almond extract
- 2 cups heavy cream

Directions
1. Combine the cream cheese, sugar, vanilla extract, and almond extract in a large mixing bowl or the bowl of a stand mixer. **2.** Fit the mixer with the whisk attachment and mix on medium speed until smooth. **3.** While the mixture is still whipping, slowly pour in the heavy cream. Stop and scrape the bottom of the bowl a couple of times while you continue whipping until the cream can hold a stiff peak.

Tips for Delectable Desserts

1. To soften hardened brown sugar, put a piece of bread in the bag. You can also microwave hardened sugar for five seconds and spoon with ease.

2. Submerge a lemon or lime in hot water or microwave for 15 seconds and double the juice you get before squeezing. Before cutting the lemon, roll it around on the counter top with the heel of your hand for even more juice. After juicing, freeze the skin in plastic wrap and have for grating to add extra flavor to a dish.

3. When slicing cheesecake or something sticky like pecan pie, try wetting the knife with hot water just before cutting. If that doesn't do the trick, try applying a bit of cooking spray to knife edge.

4. Eggs are easier to separate when cold. When separating eggs, break them into a funnel. The whites will go through and egg yolk will stay in the funnel.

5. Add moistness and taste to any chocolate cake—homemade or from a box—with a spoonful of white distilled vinegar.

6. If you want a box cake to taste like it's from a bakery, add three or four eggs instead of one or two and add a cup of sour cream.

7. To keep frosting from sugaring (getting crusty), add a drop of white distilled vinegar. It will also help keep white frosting white and shiny.

8. If your cake recipe calls for nuts, heat them first in the oven; then dust with flour before adding to the batter to keep them from settling to the bottom of the pan.

9. Keep cake mixes (spice, yellow, white, chocolate, German chocolate, angel food) on hand for a quick dessert or the base for another great offering. Add apple sauce to spice cake, pudding mix to chocolate cake, pineapples and brown sugar to the yellow mix for pineapple upside-down cake. Turn pieces of angel food cake into delicious dippers with chocolate fondue, and a white cake mix into dump cake or trifle. For those who have tried to bake a Dump Cake, here is an easy offering. In a greased 9 x 12" pan, spread 1 can of spiced apple pie filling and 1 can of crushed pineapple and mix gently; sprinkle evenly 1 yellow cake mix over the filling; then sprinkle evenly over the cake mix either chopped walnuts or pecans. Lastly, pour over nuts 1 stick of melted butter. Bake for 45 minutes on 350° oven. Serve hot with whipped cream or vanilla ice cream.

DRINKS

"Though water and green tea are the two best drinks to consume, we don't always choose our beverages wisely. Most commercial soft drinks are low in nutrition and high in sugar, and their diet counterpart is laced with aspartame, the culprit for a failing short-term memory among other terrible side effects. Healthy alternatives and delicious concoctions not only take us back to our childhood but also feed our body and soul." Linda

Blueberry Slush

"My daughter Tricia created this drink. She would whip up a batch, and we would sip on it while cuddled up on the sofa to watch a movie. It is delicious and has lots of antioxidants." Linda

Ingredients
8 oz. white grape juice

½ to 1 cup (depending on how thick you want your drink to be) frozen blueberries

2 tsp. sugar or stevia (a natural substitute for sugar)

5 ice cubes

Directions
Blend ingredients until ice turns to slush. Serve immediately.

Lemonade

"Save this recipe for the sad day when your economy goes sour, the jobless rate goes south, and entrepreneurship seems the only way to survive. Here are the makings of a successful lemonade stand! Or just let this good drink highlight your summer hospitality. Yes, there are all sorts of inexpensive faux lemon mixes, but that's exactly the reason why this classic formula is so much appreciated." Lael

Ingredients
1 cup sugar

1 cup fresh lemon juice

4 cups cold water

½ lemon, thinly sliced

Mint sprigs

Directions
1. In a pitcher, combine sugar, juice, and water and stir until sugar is dissolved. Chill. **2.** Then serve in glasses topped with lemon slices and mint sprigs.

Variation
10 cups tea, ¾ cup sugar, 6 oz. frozen lemonade

Cappuccino Ice

"I recall being more thrilled with the invention of instant coffee than I was with man's first walk on the moon. That, of course, was many years before Starbucks started its "real" coffee craze, but the instant variety still has an honored place in my pantry. This is one of many good ways to use it." Lael

Ingredients

½ cup low-fat cappuccino yogurt (or any coffee-flavored yogurt)
¼ tsp. instant coffee
¼ cup water
1 cup ice

Directions

1. Blend all the ingredients in a blender until the ice has turned to slush. **2.** Serve immediately.

Variation:

Ingredients

⅔ cup chocolate syrup, chilled
2 cups cold coffee
2 cups vanilla ice cream
Ice cubes or crushed ice
1 tsp. cinnamon (optional)
Whipped topping (optional)

Directions

1. Place syrup and coffee in a blender container. Cover and blend on high speed. **2.** Add ice cream, then cover and blend until smooth. Serve at once over ice. **3.** Top with whipped topping and ground cinnamon, if desired.

Creamsicle Ice Cream Punch

"All I have to do is check out the ingredients of this recipe to remind myself of summer and the wonderful jingly music of the neighborhood ice-cream truck. Add a jigger or two of vodka or gin and you have the X-rated adult version." Lael

Ingredients
1, 6 oz. can frozen orange juice concentrate
1 tsp. vanilla
2 scoops vanilla ice cream
½ cup sugar
6 ice cubes

Directions
1. Whip all ingredients in blender. **2.** Serve immediately.

Fruit Smoothie

"I thought I didn't like smoothies until I stumbled on this recipe tucked under the cover of a commercial yogurt container. The combination sounded so odd, I had to try it and I've hooked a good number of house guests on it since. I have varied this recipe to suit my personal taste and allow my guests to do the same, and I use my bullet blender which makes individual servings." Lael

Ingredients
1 cup frozen raspberries or strawberries
1 cup apple juice
1 cup vanilla yogurt

Additions: honey if plain yogurt is used.

Directions
1. Put frozen berries in blender and top with yogurt and apple juice. **2.** Cover and blend until smooth.

Holiday Eggnog

"The knee-jerk reaction is to buy this ready-made, but there is no substitute for doing it yourself, especially with guests looking on." Lael

Ingredients

12 eggs, separated
½ cup sugar
3 cups milk
1 cup heavy cream, whipped
½ tsp. nutmeg
½ tsp. cinnamon

Additions: 1 cup brandy, rye, whisky, or bourbon and 1 cup rum.

Directions

1. Beat egg yolks until thick and lemon-colored. **2.** Beat in sugar, gradually. Then stir in brandy (or substitute) and rum. **3.** Cover and chill. **4.** Just before serving, beat egg whites stiff. **5.** Add milk to egg yolk mixture and then fold in egg whites and whipped cream. **6.** Sprinkle with spices and serve.

Orange Julius for Real

"The first time I tasted this wonderful substitute for breakfast, I was overlooking the Pacific Ocean on a sunny morning from the patio of a mansion owned by good friends in South Laguna Beach, California. Today, the absolute pleasure of this memory charms me every bit as much of the taste of this great discovery does." Lael

Ingredients

4 cups fresh orange juice
   (frozen can be substituted
   but do not use canned juice)
1 fresh raw egg

Directions

1. If you are using frozen orange juice, reconstitute it as directed on the can. Place in blender. Add egg and whip up. **2.** Serve immediately. This doesn't store well, but you probably won't have leftovers to worry about.

Ice Cream Soda and Floats

"At age 16, I got my dream job running a soda fountain in Gilmanton, New Hampshire, and I've never quite recovered from that experience. About once a summer, I succumb to terminal nostalgia and mix up this wonderful recipe from those happy times. Most of today's generation, who have never tasted an ice cream soda, are immediately smitten and with good reason." *Lael*

"When I was young, my grandmother would dress me up (and that included a hat, gloves, and patent leather shoes in those days) and take me to downtown D.C. for a special treat. We would ride the trolley car, visit my grandfather at the Victory House, one of the three hotels he built, and stop at the corner soda fountain. The bar where we ate gleamed and the stools spun round and round, but the pièce de résistance was the root beer float. Mr. Santini made both ice cream and root beer from scratch, and I tell you there was nothing like that drink or the special memories created on those days with my grandmother." *Linda*

Ingredients

8 T. cream
4 T. chocolate or strawberry syrup
8 small scoops ice cream

1.8 oz. bottle of club soda
4 maraschino cherries (optional)
Whipped cream to top

Directions

1. Put 2 T. of cream and 1 T. or more syrup in each glass.
2. Add 2 scoops of ice cream to each glass.
3. Pour about ¼ cup soda into each glass and mash together slightly. Then fill rest of glass with soda and stir a couple of times.
4. Top with whipped cream and cherries and serve with straws and long-handled spoons for additional stirring.

Variation

Ice cream floats are made by adding scoops of ice cream to bubbling drinks like root beer, colas, or orange and strawberry soda. Vanilla or cherry syrup can be added to taste or just a dash of vanilla extract to enliven plain colas. A straw is a must.

Mulled Cider

"This recipe goes back to jolly old England and was fueled with more than a dot of dark rum. Some historians suggest that its origins are in a Christmas drink called wassail, which was made from roasted apples. Whatever its ancestry, mulled cider remains a very good idea, especially on cold night. A bit of dark rum will ward off the chill." Lael

Ingredients

2 qts. apple cider
¼ cup packed brown sugar
⅛ tsp. ground ginger
2 cinnamon sticks
1 tsp. whole cloves

Directions

Pour cider in pot, add spices and warm over low heat for an hour.

Strawberry Cream Punch

"This is a delicious punch to serve during the holidays or whenever you entertain. It looks beautiful, too, in a crystal or glass punch bowl. This is the one I make for the bridal and baby showers I give." Linda

Ingredients

20 oz. pineapple juice
½ cup sugar
½ qt. strawberry ice cream
1¼ qt. ginger ale
1¼ cups water
3 oz. can of frozen pink lemonade

Directions

Mix ingredients in a punch bowl and serve.

Drinks

Tips for Concocting Drinks with Ease

1. To make decorative ice cubes, pop in a small sprig of mint or lemon balm in each space in an ice cube tray before freezing.
2. Buttermilk substitute—combine 1 tablespoon of lemon juice or white vinegar with milk to make a cup.
3. Coconut milk substitute—combine 1 tsp. of coconut essence with milk to make a cup.
4. Almond and cashew milk are not considered dairy and are a great milk substitute. They are nutritious, have fewer calories and are good for those who are lactose intolerant.
5. If you're making anything coffee-infused or chocolatey, use ice cream in your drinks. Frappés, milkshakes, and even frozen alcoholic drinks like White Russians are more spectacular. Ice cream can turn a piña colada or strawberry margarita into something that tastes like sherbet.
6. When you're making blender drinks, do not add ice cubes until the last moment before serving to avoid excessive melting. Make sure you have the correct ratio of ice to drink contents. Best to start with about one quarter ice to other ingredients. If your drink doesn't come out thick enough, add more ice and blend again. Build up the speed on your blender gradually, especially for creamy drinks, which can get over-blended and come out too thin.
7. To make a gorgeous ice ring for your punches, bring distilled water to a boil. Let cool and pour into ice cube trays; freeze until solid. Bring 6 more cups distilled water to a boil; let cool. Arrange 12–14 halved grapefruit slices or large strawberries in an 8"-diameter tube pan. Add the ice cubes (this will help keep fruit from floating) and fill tube pan with water. Freeze until solid.
8. For a great sherbet punch, start with a cold punch bowl. That will ensure that your punch stays the right consistency for longer. Figure about 1 large scoop of sherbet per person.
9. Healthy smoothies are not difficult. A great vegetable smoothie includes 1 cup water or apple juice, 1 pear, cored and sliced, 1 apple, cored and sliced, 1 cup fresh spinach, 1 tsp. ground cinnamon and ½ cup ice. Blend and pour.
10. Refreshing summer drinks can be healthy, too. Don't give your children or guests drinks laden with sugar or aspartame. Satisfy sweet cravings with fresh fruit in nutritious smoothies. Blend 1 cup chopped carrot, 1 banana, 1 peeled kiwi, 1 apple—peeled, cored and sliced, 1 cup chopped pineapple, and 1 cup ice cubes.

Acknowledgements

We are grateful to the following people for helping us to bring this labor of love to a reality!

- Thanks to Aubrey Anderson, Phil Garrett, Rebecca Eskildsen, and Jennifer McCord at our publisher, Epicenter Press, for encouraging us to spend as much time writing down all our "kitchen stories" as we did collecting all our recipes.
- We so appreciate Lauren Taylor of Arlington, Texas. Her design of the cover is just fabulous, and she shot all the included photographs. Once Linda's publication production student and her editor-in-chief, Linda feels very much like a proud mama of this now amazing professional.
- Madeleine Dao of Arlington, Texas created the Kitchen Stories Cookbook Website. Another of Linda's amazing Editors-in-Chief, Maddie was the best of all her designers and is one of most responsible and hard-working human beings she knows.
- Rosalie L'Ecuyer served as our editor with distinction.
- Ann Higgins, Diana Strong and Gillian Smythe proved amazing proof readers.
- Thanks also to Ann Higgins for her Yummy Cake recipe and to Gloria Morris for the pie recipes that she kindly lent us from her book *Southern Sundries*.
- Thanks to Lael's highly diversified nieces; Susan and Nancy James, Judy Morgan, Jill Mason, and Pam Groswald for their encouragement and testing.
- And last but certainly not least, thanks to Linda's son, Derek Altoonian, who is not only a great cook himself, but also the most discerning and appreciative eater. It was he who encouraged Linda to begin this massive and exciting project.

Appendix: Foodie Autobiographies

Linda Altoonian

I was raised in Silver Spring, Maryland, a lush, green town painted pretty in the springtime with pink and white dogwood trees, flaming red azaleas bushes, and fragrant jasmine that climbed up picket fences and over anything in its path. As kids, we ran barefoot in the silky grass of our huge back yard, explored the rushing waters of Rock Creek Park that ran through both Maryland and Washington, D.C., and caught fireflies at night to twinkle in our glass jars.

Summer was hot and humid, but there was ample compensation. We climbed the mulberry and apple trees that dotted our back yard and ate until our tummies protruded and our hands were purple with mulberry juice. We swarmed around the milkman when he delivered to our front door the creamy liquid that we downed straight from the bottles, and when we heard the bells of the ice cream truck, the entire neighborhood hopped on bikes and raced to the top of the hill where he would stop. We colored our tongues red with strawberry popsicles and slurped cream cycles of various sweet flavors. My suburban neighborhood was a perfect page from Americana at its best.

My family's home was a lively place, two parents, three active daughters (I was the oldest and most driven and responsible—I'll blame first-child syndrome) and one dog. My quiet dad didn't have a chance in our emotional and often crazy abode, but he was brilliant and taught me a love of baseball and books. Both would be critical to my future writing career, my desire for fair play, and my need to explore the world.

From the time we were young, we were actively involved in our schools, church, and Girl Scouts, where I was introduced to my first outdoor cooking. At six years of age, I considered S'mores to be the perfect food, and who wouldn't love the gooey marshmallow and melted chocolate smashed between two fresh graham crackers. The other delicacy I learned to make was a Frito pie, truly a delight in a small package, and it was an easy recipe—open package, pour in chili, top with shredded cheese, and dig in. As we advanced in Scouts, the cooking experiences and recipes became increasingly more difficult, but I loved cooking over an open fire and having only a few gadgets to ease the process.

It had been a challenge to cook outdoors, but it was also an adventure for me that translated into food experimentation. As early as twelve, I was mixing up concoctions for my dad to use as a meat marinade and as a basting sauce when he grilled. Pretty soon my uncles and neighbors were asking for the recipes because all that was available at the grocery store was one fairly blasé, tomato-based barbecue sauce. If only my family had bottled the unique sauces I created, we could have made a fortune.

My parents had an open invitation policy, so we always had "company" including our many friends, grandparents, aunts, uncles, and cousins, all of whom lived ten minutes away in various directions. We also included a myriad of loners who didn't have family to celebrate holidays and special occasions, an absolutely horrifying situation to my large extended family who loved to eat, drink, and be merry together every single weekend.

This preoccupation with entertaining came from my roots. I am of Armenian ancestry, a pure blood on both sides of the family, and the second generation to be born in America. My grandparents, both of whom were educated and very well off in the "old country", barely escaped being killed during the Turkish genocide of 1915. They landed on Ellis Island with nothing left but their pride and determination. They began anew, learned English, and launched a successful hotel business in Washington, D.C. They soon earned the American dream—a huge home in Chevy Chase (where all the Senators and Representatives lived), founded an Armenian church in which to worship, and celebrated the freedom to flourish without fear in a new country they loved and served well.

My amazing grandparents had come as poor immigrants, joined the melting pot of many other ethnic groups, and introduced America to their unique cuisine and customs including the importance of a belief in God, hard work, a well-made meal, and hospitality. Whenever someone entered their home, a table was set immediately with bowls of steaming delicacies. The men drank shots of whiskey or highballs, and the women chatted about the dishes that the "company" had brought. One never went empty-handed to someone's house. When I was young, I thought surely it was a law. Even today, I feel compelled to take a hostess gift. Usually it is homemade paklava, an Armenian version of baklava, a delicate dessert made from Phyllo dough, butter, walnuts and cinnamon, covered by a simple sugar syrup.

At the end of the meal, a strong, thick Turkish coffee was served. Making and serving it in demitasse cups from a silver tray was a rite of passage for the young girls in the family. It was a proud moment when we were asked to make that coffee for the first time. When I was young, I didn't like the taste too much, but I would down a cup so my grandmother would "read my future" in the drippings of the overturned cup.

Every Sunday, the whole family (seventeen of us and whatever friends we decided to include that day) would gather for lively conversation, games, and shish kebab (lamb cubes marinated in wine, onions, and garlic) that was so delicious we kids could hardly wait for the skewers to come off the hot grill. That was only one dish, however, on a table laden with offerings. Mezza, appetizers including fat, black olives, tart feta cheese, spiced meats shaved into thin slices and flat, crunchy bread, were served first. Accompanying the grilled lamb and vegetables, would be rice pilaf, homemade yogurt, stuffed grape leaves, tabouli, and cheese boregs that melted in my mouth. Other delicious vegetable dishes and desserts varied from Sunday to Sunday.

Ours was basically a Mediterranean diet but was uplifted with whatever dish my grandmother created from scratch or decided to cook from her Armenian cookbook that I still use when I am making the most difficult dishes. Grandma was a master in the kitchen, and it was from her that I really learned to cook. She was fearless about adding new spices to an old favorite, or using an ingredient as a base no one else would think of. Her rose-petal jelly pops to my mind. In those days, hedges, instead of 8-foot fences separated properties, and she planted hundreds of red rose bushes as the soft and fragrant border surrounding her home. Her rose jelly was delicious on Armenian flat bread spread with cream cheese. Because I stayed at my grandparents often, I became her most ardent student. She taught me by example and by putting the knife or mixing spoon in my hand.

My grandmother planted many fruit trees in her yard. Her peach tree yielded a brandy so fine that it was saved for very special moments. The first time I tasted the brandy was after I had, for the first time, beaten my grandfather at backgammon, a national pastime for Armenians raised to art form. The pivotal occasion called for only the best celebration. I felt so grown up as I drank the luscious, liquid amber that my grandfather poured with pride into crystal goblets. The taste was magical. Even Winston Churchill once said that his favorite brandy of all came from the uniquely delicious fruits of Armenia.

I was a really lucky girl. I enjoyed the pleasures and the lessons of two very different worlds. I was an Armenian who learned about the importance of a loving family, the necessity of a great work ethic and pride in a job done well, and the disdain of failure. As a proud American, I loved our freedoms, our opportunities, our collective conscience, and our lifestyle, which was always exciting.

I'm not sure how we managed with three teenage girls, one bathroom, and one car, but we did for a long time. Unlike today, we weren't terrified to skip through the woods to our elementary school, and there was no aversion to riding the bus, often over mountains of snow to the junior and senior high schools, where I was very much a top dog. President of this and secretary of that, I was ultimately voted the person who had *Done Most for the School*. That Senior High Superlative aptly described my desire to impact whatever world I was operating in and to change for the better anything I thought was in need of fixing.

Attending the University of Maryland in College Park during the late 60s and early 70s gave me ample opportunity to be involved in righting wrongs. Just fifteen minutes outside of Washington, D.C., I was in the middle of it all—demonstrating against the Vietnam War while the National Guard combed our campus, fighting in the women's movement to break the glass ceiling, and protesting for equal rights for black Americans. Every class and every day brought new adventures to our campus—intellectually and socially. I was too naive to really understand the possible danger of some of our activities (we all thought ourselves immortal) until several prominent leaders were assassinated and four students were killed on the Kent State campus. Those were emotional times and pivotal moments in history and in my life, and I would not have traded one minute.

I married an Armenian boy from New Jersey after graduating college. Called the Garden State, Jersey offered the most flavorful vegetables I have ever tasted, silver queen corn and tomatoes in particular, and our home's proximity to Philadelphia allowed for both eating the best deli food outside of New York City and tasting and trying to make for the first time many new dishes unique to the area: gooey calzones, soft pretzels smeared with spicy mustard, and Philly cheese steaks were a few of my favorites.

My marriage heralded many firsts in my life—teaching for the first time, buying and decorating our first home, giving parties for our friends and family, and cooking all the meals even when I was teaching full time and completing my master's degree. Those were still the times that women did it all— brought home the bacon and cooked it, too!

That was when I really honed my cooking skills. Though generally whatever I served was a hit, there were a couple of mishaps along the way. I remember "baking" my first London Broil, which I thought took as long to cook as a regular roast. At the end of two hours, it looked and tasted like shoe leather, and for a girl who loves medium rare meat, it was particularly awful.

I broiled it quickly from then on and learned how to make a delicious brown sauce that complemented it perfectly.

My husband's mother was a great cook and introduced me to lots of new and more sophisticated dishes. From her, I learned how to make dishes like Beef Wellington, complex sauces and dressings, pickled vegetables and cheesecake from scratch. Though my mother hadn't really liked to cook (she was an artist at heart), her fare had been simple but good, except for a number of dishes that were absolutely stellar including—her turkey stuffing, potato salad, and the grape leaves (grown in her own garden) that she stuffed. I still make all of her dishes just as she did.

I became Earth Mother when I began to have my children (for whom I quit work to raise full time)—natural deliveries to avoid exposing my babies to drugs, nursing each of them for a year to increase intellect and protect against disease, and making all their food from scratch—no jarred food or formula for my kids. Buying chemical-free produce and meats, steaming vegetables lightly to avoid losing vitamins and minerals, and sweetening with nature's bounty (prunes and apple sauce) characterized my cooking style long before it became popular to do so. It was fun to concoct the dishes that both my husband and my kids enjoyed.

My last training ground in culinary delights came after my two children were successfully launched and on their own, and I was back to work after fifteen years of homemaking, volunteering and civic advocacy—*first* as the Editor-in-Chief of numerous national magazines that always featured unique recipes that I loved to acquire, (including the ONLY authorized magazine about the life of one of baseball's greats, Mickey Mantle, which I dedicated to my dad), *then* as a syndicated columnist for the local newspaper and author of a book based on that column, and *finally* as a journalism and publication production teacher taking students on educational trips throughout the Europe that I had avidly studied and loved from afar all my life.

I will skip the pure pleasure I found in the art, history and culture coming to life for me at every turn in all the countries I have toured extensively and will concentrate only on the food. It was in Italy that I learned how to make the best pizza and marinara sauce ever, and I learned about the magic of lemons in various dishes served in Pompeii and Capri. I couldn't get enough of the sangria and paella in Spain, and I adored the fried milk and churros dipped in chocolate. In France, I questioned the chefs until they divulged what made their sauces so special, and in Germany, I learned the art of making luscious noodles from scratch. In Ireland, I fell in love with my first Shepherd's Pie and in Morocco, I learned invaluable lessons about the infinite number of spices available to use not only to season food, but also to improve health and literally save lives.

Everywhere I travel there is something to learn about life and the food that sustains it. Food is the common denominator among people all over the world—we all need it to live. We all take pride in serving it well prepared, and we all express our love and appreciation of others through what we serve them.

The world is a magical place, and I have been a passionate wanderer who's traveled to over 45 states and 35 countries. I have seized every opportunity to challenge myself, to learn something new, and to give something back. I have experienced the cultural diversity that impacts attitude and lifestyle and can be divisive, and I have experienced the joy and creativity of the human spirit and the thread of hope that binds us all.

We hope you enjoy our comfort food recipes, both homegrown and brought to America by all the courageous immigrants who pulled up their roots, packed up their traditions, and braved the high seas. We have tried to keep them simple to make (really, how can you beat needing only six ingredients), delicious to eat, and a prompt to remember, which I have done fondly throughout.

Because my style of cooking is very much "a little of this and a little of that," my children insisted that I finally measure and note how I make what, so they can duplicate the dishes. It was for them that I began this project, so writing this has been a real labor of love both for my family and for the opportunity to work with my writing partner, Lael Morgan, whom I have known well and have admired greatly for over ten years. Her generosity is boundless and her desire to help others is an inspiration. I am grateful for having known her and now for having worked with her.

Lael Morgan

As a child, I was so enchanted with the open fields and endless woods where I was raised in rural Maine that I tried unsuccessfully to run away when my family moved to its capital city, Augusta, in 1974. Gone were the wild strawberry, blueberry, and raspberry patches I had enjoyed in season. Gone was the tent in which my brother and I had lived from early spring until late fall when our parents insisted we spend time indoors. Gone were the snowy hills down which we slid on Mom's silver-plated tea trays—wedding presents for which she could find no better use in our remote retreat. Gone were our chickens, our huge vegetable garden, and the neighbors who churned our butter and let me try to ride their pigs. Although it wasn't my decision at age eleven, I traded all those things that I loved for indoor plumbing, Augusta's beautiful Lithgow Library, and a nearby grocery store called A&P where I soon discovered the joy of grocery shopping.

My brother will tell you our mother was a wonderful cook, but he is two years younger than I and does not remember the early days when she was still "practicing." Her bread, even then, was tasty but once cooled you could easily throw a loaf through any wall. Not in a dozen tries could she bake lemon meringue pie without the crust rising to the top. The concept of rare meat never did occur to her. However, she would tackle anything from baking ice cream (Baked Alaska) to roasting a woodchuck (which actually isn't too bad). I admired her pluck and tenacity, and pretty soon I came to admire her cooking, too, which is why I quickly followed in her footsteps, benefiting greatly from her tolerance of *my* early culinary disasters.

Most of my experiments were pretty simple because traditional New England dishes seldom involve more than six spices—salt, pepper, cinnamon, nutmeg, cloves, and poultry seasoning. Finally, Mom discovered something very new called pizza and, with it, oregano. Then, when *Life Magazine* did a feature on Chinese cooking which none of us had tried, she allowed me to test those recipes. Having no idea how work-intensive it would be, I grandly announced a menu of Egg Rolls, Shrimp Fried Rice, Beef Chop Suey, Fried Shrimp Curls, and Sweet and Sour Pork.

Sadly, working all day, I completed only the Egg Rolls and Fried Rice by supper time; however, the family was intrigued. Patiently they went through the rest of my menu at the rate of one dish a day and ended up hooked on soy sauce.

By 1952, I was experienced enough so that Mother "hired" me as our cook while she, now a social worker, was off trying to make sense out of Maine's abysmal poverty. My contract specified that I was to receive the then-generous sum of $25 per week to purchase groceries and my wages would be any money that was left over when the next grocery purchase payment arrived. The problem was that I loved rich food and usually exhausted our budget early. My brother, who had escaped to work at a Boy Scout camp but had Thursdays off, complained loudly about having always to eat beans while hearing wild rumors about the steaks and cakes I'd served earlier in the week.

My freshman year in college found me living in a lovely dorm in Boston with probably the best cook I'd ever met running its dining room. I never did succeed in discovering her secret for producing light, delectably flavored French toast, but one roommate taught me how to cook toasted cheese sandwiches with the laundry room flat iron without setting the dorm on fire, and the father of another, a genteel Southern doctor, introduced me to oysters on the half shell.

When I could no longer afford the dorm (or oysters), another student and I rented a gilded library in a turn-of-the-century Beacon Street townhouse whose owner was down on his luck. It came with a beautiful hard wood floor, rococo ceiling, and an ornate niche with the life-sized alabaster bust of an unnamed goddess next to a two burner hot plate. In that era before the marketing of Ramen noodles, when restaurants never provided "doggie bags," our $20 per week food budget was a stretch. Our staples were "Spanish rice," a recipe we still enjoy, and whatever might be on sale.

I had assumed my roommate, being as bright as she was beautiful, could cook. After several tries at boiling rice—one that ended with her actually making it explode like popcorn—she said she'd take over the dishwashing in our tiny bathroom sink if I would man the hotplate. Later, she married a Greek national and began producing wonderfully complicated concoctions with grape leaves and strange spices. She also became one of the best sous chefs with whom I've ever worked, which has since kept me from giving up on anyone. But through our student tenure, she scrubbed the dishes and was graciously uncomplaining about my low-budget cooking experiments.

I married into Boston society but, happily, my mother-in-law came from basic beginnings and was a marvelous cook. What we lacked in rapport was eased by our mutual joy of working in the kitchen. I still treasure what she taught me, which gave me a foot in two worlds.

As newlyweds, it was the goal of my husband, a former Air Force pilot, and I to finish working our way through school and then save enough money to buy a boat and sail around the world. By 1959, we had earned our diplomas from Boston University and moved to Alaska where wages were high. Having been raised in rural Maine, I felt very much at home in that northern state where wild game, fish, fiddlehead greens, and berries were staples. In fact, we did so well at living off the land while holding corporate jobs that we saved enough to buy a rich man's yacht in just four years, and headed for the high seas.

Before we left, a friend who collected recipe books asked if I would buy one for her in every exotic place I visited, and she financed that request. I never bothered to thank her because it didn't dawn on me until much later that she'd forever changed my life for the better.

Being out of touch with the *New York Times* best sellers list, I read every cookbook I purchased for her from cover to cover before I dutifully mailed it north. Inspired by wonderful local recipes, I became a fan of grouper and goat meat, grew hopelessly addicted to pigeon peas, and learned to make soursop ice cream out of a wonderful but scary looking fruit I would have otherwise avoided.

My husband was no foodie. His second wife (a good friend) has accused him of having the "palate of a seagull." But he was endlessly patient and often quite amused by watching me attempt the sad but basic cooking tasks of low budget sailing like trying to get conch out of their beautiful shells and cooking turtles.

After a year of sailing the Bahamas, we ran out of money and stopped to earn more in the Virgin Islands which had a wonderful charter boat fleet. Being an era when propane and electricity were not readily available and microwaves had yet to be invented, most of the elegant meals the charter-boat wives served wealthy guests were cooked on cranky primus stoves, which was all we had, too. What we didn't have were the recipes they created to cope with this hindrance. Learning from them how to "bake" bread in a pressure cooker and keep a barbeque relatively steady on a heaving deck made low-budget yachting in our old, 36-foot schooner a delight, and we spent two more years on the high seas, before sailing back to Alaska via Hawaii.

Separating from my husband in 1965, I got a dream job on the *Juneau Empire*, in Alaska's capital. As its only full-time reporter and photographer, I covered everything from politics to sports and visiting dignitaries, like Craig Claiborne—famed food writer for the *New York Times*. My husband, with whom I remained the best of friends, went east to write a book about our trip while I spent my off-hours working on a boating cookbook featuring my favorite charter boat recipes and other exotic fare. Discovering that I'd neglected to save directions for cooking shark, I posted a notice in the paper asking for help which prompted a fine culinary contribution from Juneau's garbage collector.

After various assignments in Alaska, I got a job at the *Los Angeles Times* in Orange County, California, where I reported on welfare mothers, Pat Nixon, migrants sans green cards, white-collar crime, and the lives of the idle rich. In the process, I fell in with a group of connoisseurs who thought nothing of spending a day and a half preparing one complicated recipe requiring a zillion weird ingredients. That was exciting. So were much simpler Mexican dishes that became my staple until I returned to Alaska to cover its indigenous people, who were trying to gain title to lands they had used and occupied for centuries.

Alaska's Natives were generally classified as Eskimos, Indians, and Aleuts but they spoke half a dozen distinctly different languages, and their lifestyles differed as wildly as the state's rugged topography which ran from arctic tundra to southern rain forests. Most lived off the land by hunting and fishing. Traveling among them, I gained the distinction of eating more endangered species than most people would ever see. I also dined on polar bear, walrus, seal, and a never-ending sea of salmon.

For three seasons, I served as an assistant cook on Inupiat whaling crews, living in tents out on the sea ice; we provided hunters with frozen, raw sheefish, boiled eider ducks, caribou stews with macaroni, and doughnuts we fried over Coleman hot plates or homemade stoves fueled with rancid seal fat. If our hunters got lucky, there would also be whale meat and muktuk which proved the subject of much joking among many non-Natives but, if cooked correctly, is truly a gourmet delicacy.

Also during this period, the Aleuts taught me two-century-old Russian recipes and the way to survive on distant beaches by eating local greens and odd looking shellfish. An Athabascan Indian hostess showed me how to "knit" fish net and her neighbor's son taught me how to catch supper and smoke leftovers. The Tlingit and Haida Indians treated me to herring and salmon specialties. The Yup'ik favored Eskimo ice cream, traditionally a colorful mixture of whipped seal oil and sweet wild berries.

Later, there was the rest of the world to investigate; the South Seas, Scotland, the Seychelle Islands, Atka, and Texas preferred. It was in Texas I encountered Linda Altoonian at a meeting of the Press Women who had just named her Teacher of the Year. We should have been talking journalism, but when we discovered our mutual passion for local foods that became a special bond.

"There is no accounting for taste," it is said, but I believe it has a lot to do with foods discovered along the trail of exciting lives, which we've both traveled most happily. Our souvenirs are cooking treasures I hope you will also enjoy in all their flavor and simplicity.

Index

Table of Contents...iii

Foreword by Stephen L. Hardin, Ph.D....v

Introduction...vii

Appetizers...1
Artichoke Dip...2
Bruschetta Cheddar...2
Cheese Ball...3
Chicken Wings Buffalo...4
Chicken Wings Far East...5
Clam Dip...6
Crab Dip...7
Deviled Eggs...8
Dill Dip...5
Easy Cheese...3
Feta Spread...9
Guacamole...11
Hummus Dip...12
Mexican Layered Dip...13
Mini Lasagna...14
Nachos...15
Phyllo Cheese...10
Salmon Mousse...16
Salsa...17
Shrimp Dip...18
Texas Caviar...19
Tips for Tasty Appetizers...20
Tortilla Roll-ups...18

Breads and Rolls...21
Banana Bread...22
Boston Brown Bread...23
Bran Muffins...24
Buttermilk Biscuits...25
Cornbread...26
Cream Biscuits...24
French Toast...27
Fried Bread...28
Hush Puppies...29
No Knead Bread...30
Popovers...31
Refrigerator Rolls...32
Resurrection Rolls...33
Sourdough Pancakes...34
Sourdough Starter...35
Spoon Bread...29
Tips for Better Bread...36

Salads...37
Artichoke and Lima Beans...38
Bean Salad...39
Caesar Salad...40
Cole Slaw...41
Cranberry and Pineapple Frozen Salad...42
Fruit Salad...43
Greek Salad...43
Macaroni and Tuna Fish...44
Mandarin Orange Salad...45
Oriental Salad...46
Pasta Salad...47

Pea Pod Imperial...48
Potato Salad...49
Spinach Salad with Fruit...50
Tips for Special Salads...58
Tomato Salad Italian...51
Waldorf Salad...48

Salad Dressings...52
Bleu Cheese...52
Creamy Italian...53
Mustard Dressing...53
Ranch Dressing...55
Russian Dressing...55
Sweet and Savory
 Vinaigrette...56
Sweetened Mayonnaise
 Dressing...57
Thousand Island Dressing...56
Traditional French Dressing...54
Vinaigrette French Dressing...54

**Soups, Stews
and Chowders...59**
Beef Stew...60
Borscht...61
Chicken Noodle Soup...62
Clam or Fish Chowder,
 New England...63
Corn Chowder...64
Cream of Crab...65
French Onion Soup...66
Lemon Egg Soup...67
Lentil Soup...68
Pea Soup...69
Potato Soup...70
Pumpkin Soup...70
Tips for Soups, Stews
 and Chowders...74
Tomato Basil Soup...71
U.S. Senate Bean Soup...72
Vegetable Soup...73

Entrees...75
Beef Brisket...76
Beef Stroganoff...77
Brunch Casserole...78
Chicken Cacciatore...79
Chicken Dinner, in Foil
 or Tin Can...80
Chicken for Dummies...81
Chicken Fried Steak...82
Chicken Parmesan...78
Chicken Salad...83
Chicken Spaghetti...84
Chili...85
Corned Beef and Cabbage...86
Croquettes...87
Dolma or Stuffed Cabbage...88
Fish Baked in Sour Cream...89
Fish Poached in Lemon Milk...90
Fried Chicken...91
Fried Chicken in the Oven...92
Ham Hocks and Black-Eyed
 Peas...93
Italian Meatballs...94
Kapusta...95
Lamb Chops...96
Lazy Lasagna...97
Macaroni and Cheese...98
Maryland Crab Cakes...99
Meatloaf...100
Pasta Alfredo...101
Pizza...102
Pork Tenderloin Roasted...103
Pot Pie...104
Quiche Lorraine...105
Ranch Roast...106
Red Flannel Hash...107
Salisbury Steak...108
Salmon Pie or Peirok in
 Russian...109
Saucy Sirloin Burgers...110

Scotch Roast...111
Shellfish Steamed...112
Shepherd's Pie...113
Sloppy Joes...114
Spaghetti Sauce...115
Spanish Rice...116
Tips for Easier Entrees...130
Tortilla Wraps...117
Turkey a la King...118
Veal Cutlets...119
Welsh Rarebit...120

Gravy, Sauces and Toppings...121
Basil Pesto...121
Brown Gravy...122
Cheese Sauce...123
Garlic Wine Sauce...124
Hollandaise Sauce...125
Horseradish Sauce...126
Mustard Crème Sauce...126
Newburg Sauce...127
Rockport Red Sauce...128
Tartar Sauce...127
White Gravy...129

Vegetable and Side Dishes...131
Acorn Squash...132
Asparagus...134
Baked Beans...135
Chicken Stuffing, in the bird...155
Corn Bake...136
Eggplant Baked...137
Eggplant Parmigiana...138
Fried Green Tomatoes...139
Fried Okra...140
Grits...140
Mashed Potatoes...141
Onion Rings in the Bag...142

Potato Pancakes...142
Potatoes Parmesan...143
Potatoes Scalloped...144
Potatoes Twice Baked...145
Rice Pilaf...148
Rice Re-do...147
Savory Squash...133
Spinach Italian...149
Squash Casserole...150
Stir-Fried Veggies...151
String Beans Almandine...152
Succotash...153
Sweet Potatoes California...146
Tips for Dealing with Vegetables...158
Turkey Stuffing, stove top...154
Wild Rice...156
Zucchini Soufflé...157

Desserts...159
Apple Brown Betty...160
Apple Pie...161
Baked Alaska...162
Bread Pudding...163
Brownies...164
Butterscotch Fudge...176
Carrot Cake...165
Cheese Cake...166
Cherry or Strawberry Rhubarb Pie...167
Chocolate Fondue...168
Chocolate Mousse Cake...169
Chocolate Pecan Squares...165
Cream Puffs...173
Creamy Pies...170
Flan...174
Golden Fruit Cake...177
Key Lime Pie...178
Lemon Bars...179
Meringue...171
Mud Pie...180

Pecan Pie...176
Piecrust (Baked)...172
Piecrust (Unbaked)...172
Pumpkin Soufflé...181
Rice Pudding...182
Rhubarb Pie...167
Strawberries Devonshire...184
Strawberry Bavarian Cream...183
Tips for Delectable
 Desserts...200
Torte...185
Traditional Chocolate
 Fudge...175
Trifle...186
Turtle Cake...182
Vanilla Custard...188
Yummy Sheet Cakes...187

Dessert Sauces...189
Chocolate Syrup...189
Fruit Sauce...190
Hard Sauce...191
Hot Caramel Sauce...193
Hot Chocolate Sauce...192
Lemon Cream Sauce...191
Praline Sauce...189
Vanilla Sauce...192

Frostings and Icings...194
Butter Cream Frosting...198
Cake and Pastry Glaze...196
Chocolate Frosting...194
Chocolate Glaze...196
Cream Cheese Frosting...195
Maple Syrup Frosting...195
Peanut Butter Frosting...197
Vanilla Frosting...197
Whipped Cream...199

Drinks...201
Blueberry Slush...202
Cappuccino Ice...203
Creamsicle Ice Cream
 Punch...204
Fruit Smoothie...204
Holiday Egg Nog...205
Ice Cream Soda and Floats...206
Lemonade...202
Mulled Cider...207
Orange Julius for Real...205
Strawberry Cream Punch...207
Tips for Concocting Drinks
 with Ease...208

Acknowledgements...209

**Appendix: Foodie
Autobiographies by
Authors...211**

Contact authors at lindaaltoonian@hotmail.com
and laelmorgan@cs.com

Find more recipes, cooking tips, and exciting contests at
www.kitchenstoriescookbook.blogspot.com

Place book orders at www.epicenterpress.com,
www.amazon.com, or www.barnesandnoble.com

Happy Eating!

Add Your Family Recipes and Stories and make this cookbook a Family Treasure

Recipe Name _____

Name of Contributor _____

Ingredients

_____ _____ _____
_____ _____ _____
_____ _____ _____
_____ _____ _____

Directions

_____
_____
_____
_____
_____
_____
_____
_____

Story

_____
_____
_____
_____
_____
_____
_____
_____

Recipe Name _____

Name of Contributor _____

Ingredients

_____ _____ _____

_____ _____ _____

_____ _____ _____

_____ _____ _____

Directions

_____

_____

_____

_____

_____

_____

_____

Story

_____

_____

_____

_____

_____

_____

_____

_____

_____

_____

Recipe Name _____

Name of Contributor _____

Ingredients

_____ _____ _____

_____ _____ _____

_____ _____ _____

_____ _____ _____

Directions

_____

_____

_____

_____

_____

_____

_____

_____

Story

_____

_____

_____

_____

_____

_____

_____

_____

_____

_____

_____

_____

Recipe Name _____

Name of Contributor _____

Ingredients

_____ _____ _____

_____ _____ _____

_____ _____ _____

_____ _____ _____

Directions

_____

_____

_____

_____

_____

_____

_____

Story

_____

_____

_____

_____

_____

_____

_____

_____

_____

_____

Recipe Name _____

Name of Contributor _____

Ingredients

_____ _____ _____

_____ _____ _____

_____ _____ _____

_____ _____ _____

Directions

_____

_____

_____

_____

_____

_____

_____

Story

_____

_____

_____

_____

_____

_____

_____

_____

_____

_____

_____